Dyslexia and Foreign Language Learning

Dyslexia and Foreign Language Learning

Elke Schneider and Margaret Crombie

David Fulton Publishers

London

David Fulton Publishers Ltd
The Chiswick Centre, 414 Chiswick High Road, London W4 5TF

www.fultonpublishers.co.uk

David Fulton Publishers is a division of Granada Learning Limited, part of Granada plc.

First published 2003

British Library Cataloguing in Publication Data
A catalogue record for this book is available from the British Library.

ISBN 1 85346 966 1

Typeset by Pracharak Technologies (P) Ltd, Madras, India
Printed and bound in Great Britain by Ashford Colour Press Ltd, Gosport, Hants

Contents

Foreword

We are indeed indebted to the authors Elke Schneider and Margaret Crombie for utilising their vast experience, in both research and practice in foreign languages, in this book. We know of no other book as concise and comprehensive in its comments, discussions and strategies for foreign language learners.

As the authors suggest, learning foreign languages (FL) can provide a challenge to children and young adults with dyslexia. This can also provide a challenge to educators who are responsible for the accommodations that can help to ensure that the potential demands of language learning are minimised for those with dyslexia.

Crombie and Schneider illustrate very clearly how this can be achieved and describe why foreign languages can be so demanding for students with dyslexia. They also highlight specific examples of the accommodations that can be made as well as considering the influence of legislation on education and dyslexia.

This book has been written following extensive research and, as the authors point out, the techniques and strategies presented in this book are relevant no matter the country or the language. They also rightly point out that foreign language learning can and should be possible for the vast majority of students. They maintain it is the right of every student to be able to attempt to learn a foreign language.

The innovative chapter on metacognition (Chapter 3) highlights the need to allow the student to take responsibility for his/her own learning and this chapter demonstrates, through utilising the findings from the fields of psychology and education, how this can be achieved. The authors provide scores of strategies to facilitate successful learning and to help the student with dyslexia achieve success. At the same time the authors highlight the responsibility of teachers to be aware of how they themselves can maximise students' potential and provide students with the opportunities for success.

There are many barriers to foreign language learning and these are explored by the authors. With this in mind they provide a sound hypothesis when they say that 'if the curriculum is geared to the needs of individual foreign language learners, including those with dyslexia, then students along the entire continuum of FL aptitude stand a good chance of success. How the curriculum is presented is important.' This provides an excellent framework of support for teachers and educators, and this book therefore must surely be an essential tool for all those engaged in foreign language learning and teaching.

The authors have taken a broad perspective focusing not only on describing the difficulties but also on constructive comments on support strategies that can promote autonomy in learning. Their message that 'the ethos of the whole school influences learning' should not be lost on educators. Students with dyslexia, regardless of their age, are particularly sensitive to conditions in their learning environments. Therefore, it is vital, as the authors suggest, that the learning environment be positive and constructive. It is also important that teachers are familiar with dyslexia, its characteristics and how success in the foreign languages classroom can be achieved by students with dyslexia. We believe this book will go a long way towards helping teachers achieve this goal.

Lindsay Peer CBE
Gavin Reid
May 2003

Introduction

This book sets out to inform foreign/second language educators and to offer support to teachers on the nature of dyslexic difficulties as they affect the learning of another language. It presents teaching and assessment strategies for those with specific language processing difficulties which are commonly associated with dyslexia. While the term 'dyslexia' is used throughout this book, the strategies presented will work well for many students, not just those who have the officially identified language processing difficulty called 'dyslexia'.

Background and definitions

Definitions of dyslexia are many and varied. The Greek root of the word does little to simplify the debate over exactly what dyslexia is. The term comes from two Greek words: *dys* (here meaning 'difficulty with') and *lexicos* or *lexis* (meaning 'words') (Doyle 1996: 69; BPS 1999: 18). This description, taken to refer to written words of a language, whether related to reading, spelling and/or writing, provides a vague indication of what is involved.

For well over a hundred years now, dyslexia has been recognised and knowledge accumulates with every year that passes. Researchers have come together from various disciplines to pool their knowledge with a mind to developing our knowledge base and improving practice for dyslexic people of all ages. Chapter 1 sets out why it is that dyslexic students find language learning particularly problematic, but it is important to state here that dyslexia exists on a continuum with every student being an individual with a different pattern of strengths and weaknesses. Although difficulties vary in severity between individuals, there is a set of common characteristics, many of which generally affect language learning (Miles 1993; Miles and Miles 1999). Even for those students whose native language has reached a very adequate standard, the learning of a foreign language can present particular challenges. Besides the difficulties of reading and spelling that are generally associated with dyslexia, there are difficulties in recognising language patterns that are presented orally. This makes the discovery of grammatical and/or lexical word patterns difficult or sometimes almost impossible without specific interventions. Poor handwriting too can affect the flow (and therefore the processing) of patterns. Difficulties can therefore be oral, auditory, kinaesthetic and visual. In short, dyslexia generally affects the oral and written language skills that are essential for success in learning a foreign language (Gerber 1993; Lerner 1997). Difficulties tend to run in families and have a genetic base manifesting themselves to varying degrees over generations.

Neurologists have studied the differences in brain structure (often unexpected variations in structures and functioning of the hemispheres of the brain) and processing (different patterns of brain activation) (Bakker 1990; Perani *et al.* 1996). While dyslexia is not curable and language processing cannot be 'fixed' by wearing tinted glasses or hearing aids, there is still much we can do to make learning easier for the dyslexic student. For the foreign language educator, dyslexia can be seen as a difficulty that slows down the 'in-brain' language processing procedure, demanding more concentration and time for processing than a non-dyslexic student will require. This results in the dyslexic student seeming to have a short concentration span for both oral and written language. In order to meet the needs of the dyslexic pupil in the language learning process, foreign language educators and parents can apply specific strategies and accommodations which have been researched and proved successful in facilitating learning and teaching in foreign languages. Test-taking and study strategies are described in later chapters and these too are an essential part of successfully tackling the language learning programme of dyslexic students.

For the purposes of this book, the dyslexia definition of Crombie (2002: 223) is used to refer to those 'who have a difficulty with literacy which results in them requiring a set of accommodations to be made to enable them to demonstrate their abilities'.

Accommodations

Accommodations in the foreign/second language classroom can then be defined as 'a set of enabling arrangements which are put in place to ensure that the dyslexic person can demonstrate their strengths and abilities, and show attainment' (Crombie 2002: 222). Accommodations could refer to the use of a reader and/or scribe to enable the person to demonstrate what they know without the necessity to read or write directly. The use of technology to produce work would be another example of an accommodation. This is further explored in later chapters of this book. The challenge when working with dyslexic people in school settings is to enable them to show what they can do, not what they cannot do, thus empowering them and including them in the classroom. This is particularly important in what often seems to be an intimidating foreign language learning situation.

The current inclusive educational philosophy is embodied in the previously described definition of dyslexia and suggests how accommodations can enable the dyslexic student, thus including them in the foreign language curriculum. This accords with the present legislation which makes discrimination on the grounds of disability illegal and requires learning to take place in the least restrictive environment and aims to emphasise a person's abilities rather than lacking skills (Disability Discrimination Act 1995). For the teacher in the classroom, the priority is to enable curricular access for any dyslexic individual in more than physical terms. To be truly included, the pupils must actively participate in all learning and teaching activities of the classroom. The foreign language classroom is no exception.

Many of the strategies discussed in the book could refer to almost any language, though the authors' experiences lie mainly in European languages. Languages that have a more pictorial script may require a different approach with multi-sensory structured teaching strategies of new letter or whole word shapes tied to sounds. Most of the principles of teaching and learning outlined in the book, however, will be very similar.

Terminology

In producing this book, the authors had considerable discussion on the terminology to use, and the differences that exist on both sides of the Atlantic. The term 'foreign language (FL)' has been used in order to include the 'dead' languages. There is no reason to assume that 'dead' languages (e.g. Latin) will present different learning challenges for dyslexic students than modern foreign languages, and no reason to assume that dyslexic students will not study a 'dead' language at some point. We also use the term 'FL educator' frequently to include teachers, tutors and lecturers. The term is used in its widest sense to cover all those involved in the education of those learning a foreign language. We do, however, use other terms as and when appropriate.

Challenges

For teachers of foreign languages, support teachers, modern languages assistants, classroom assistants, auxiliaries, dyslexic learners and parents there are many challenges to be addressed. There is no guarantee of success, but some of the greatest barriers to success are negative attitudes. With a positive outlook, an emphasis on achievement and a variety of strategies to try out if any one technique is unsuccessful, the outcomes have a good chance of being favourable. Even if the student is never able to produce brilliantly written language or to read particularly well, confidence in listening, understanding and speaking the language of choice must be the main aims of our teaching to dyslexic students who already struggle to read and write in their native language. If we can also make the language learning process personally meaningful, motivating and fun for the learner, we can truly congratulate ourselves and our students on a successful outcome.

Chapter 1

Success in a Mainstream Foreign Language Classroom

Dyslexic pupils in inclusive foreign language courses

In any foreign language classroom there will be a variety of students with various linguistic strengths and weaknesses. All are entitled to attend and participate in foreign language classes. Thus, today's foreign language educator faces the entire spectrum of foreign language learners from very good or gifted to very poor in one and the same class and has the task to meet all their individual needs in the 'least restrictive environment'. This situation is referred to as 'inclusive learning' and has become the law in many Western countries (e.g. the United Kingdom, Germany and the USA). Young people today are entitled to be included in mainstream classrooms regardless of the type and degree of their difficulty. For the majority of pupils with disabilities, this is undoubtedly most beneficial. With regard to foreign language learning and dyslexia, however, there are FL educators, administrators and parents who would doubt whether students with dyslexia should even attempt a foreign language, given their difficulties with processing language and identifying language patterns on their own. For teachers who believe in the rights of all young people to be included with their peer group, to gain knowledge of foreign culture and language, and to enhance their professional opportunities in the future, the dilemma is not whether to include children with difficulties, but how to include them successfully through appropriate accommodations. Unfortunately, training in accommodations for students with language processing difficulties has not been a routine part of teacher education in most foreign language teacher education programmes. Despite these challenges, we owe it to our pupils to give them opportunities that will help them realise their potential in a foreign language environment.

In order to succeed in this endeavour, FL educators have to realise that inclusion is not about staying the pace whatever the costs. While dyslexic individuals may be physically included in an FL language classroom, they may themselves opt out of involvement and develop negative attitudes within that environment if the curriculum or the ways of presenting it are inappropriate to their ways of learning. Failure to learn and true inclusion, however, are not compatible, and thus this book introduces interested FL educators to a variety of strategies and gives background information essential to developing a positive learning environment for dyslexic students in their inclusive classrooms. The recommendations suggested have been researched thoroughly and represent the most up-to-date information available on FL teaching to dyslexic students. The language teaching suggestions were designed predominantly with alphabetic languages in mind. They are also adjustable to any age group. All ideas have been compiled in the attempt to support the recent noticeable increased interest in and awareness of the need for special accommodations for students with dyslexia in language learning courses since the First International Conference on Multilingualism and Dyslexia took place in Manchester, England, in 1999. This conference was supported by the British Dyslexia Association, the International Dyslexia Association and the European Dyslexia Association and since then well-attended biannual conferences have served to illustrate growing awareness of, and willingness to gain well-informed, research-based information about, improving teaching and learning environments for dyslexic students and their FL educators.

There has been no attempt to differentiate between pictographic scripts and those more geared to the European context. The term 'dyslexia' is generally associated with reading, spelling and writing difficulties. However, dyslexia generally has wider connotations, and difficulties affect various aspects of language processing generally. Techniques and strategies presented in this book are relevant, no matter which country or language we consider.

Reasons for language learning difficulties

In the eighties and early nineties, some educators thought they had found the answer to any problems that dyslexic students were likely to face. Because the difficulties were based on an assumption of oral and receptive competence in their native language when compared to reading and writing difficulties, it was assumed that dyslexic pupils would be able to speak and understand a foreign language without undue problems (Crombie 1995). It was assumed that the dyslexic student would be able to listen and speak in a foreign language just fine because he or she managed to perform well in listening and speaking in the native language. Recommendations then were to omit the reading and writing elements of the language to avoid the perceived areas of difficulty.

Dyslexic pupils would then be able to cope with the foreign language just as they did in English. This did not, however, take account of other areas that dyslexic young people find problematic, and therefore the anticipated overall success was seldom achieved. While the early anticipations of success in language learning have since been challenged, this is not to say that dyslexic students cannot meet success, and some teachers have celebrated such achievements. This book sets out to correct misconceptions about language learning and dyslexia, to challenge some of the views held and to propose methods by which teachers can maximise the effect of their efforts in enabling young people's success in language learning. Illustrations are given in this chapter of successful students' experiences in order that those who are keen to meet the needs of dyslexic students might feel encouraged and gain confidence to be able to help.

Dyslexia is defined slightly differently in different countries. Even within one country definitions vary (British Psychological Society 1999; Eames 2002). It is safe to say though that dyslexia is understood as a language processing difficulty to varying degrees that affects mainly reading and writing in letter, number and/or musical symbols. These difficulties occur because of differing abilities of the brain to process auditory and/or visually presented information. While dyslexia cannot be cured, specific accommodations through professional teaching can provide the dyslexic individual with successful coping strategies (Augur 1993: 1; Birsh 1999).

Generally, poorly performing FL students with dyslexia should not be accused of lack of motivation or even be blamed for their difficulties.

Rather, as researchers Ganschow and Sparks point out in many of their studies (Ganschow *et al.* 1998), it is the linguistic difficulties that cause frustration and low motivation to continue with FL studies. This is especially true if the FL educator has not had training opportunities in the identification of dyslexic students' needs nor been introduced to successful accommodation strategies. Due to lack of such background information, the underlying difficulties that affect dyslexic people often go unrecognised.

Underlying problems associated with dyslexia can cause many of the frustration and emotional problems that inhibit dyslexic learners. Factors such as poor phonological processing skills, weak short-term and working memory, word-finding difficulties, slower speed of processing, difficulties with auditory perception and discrimination and/or auditory sequencing problems, automaticity problems, difficulties with syntax and grammar cause further problems. These are frequently exacerbated by low self-esteem and motivation. All these contribute to present a major challenge to both the dyslexic learner and the FL teacher. While dyslexic students exhibit a pattern of such difficulties, they do not necessarily exhibit all of them (Miles 1993). This differential pattern of difficulties means that students will not all respond in exactly the same way to chosen accommodation activities presented in this book. Each student has a unique profile of strengths and weaknesses. It is necessary then to get to know the students and their particular strengths through regular dialogue and an agreement between student and teacher to experiment with a variety of strategies to find the ones that work best for each individual in order to maximise chances of success. Success can only be achieved if there is harmony between the teacher and the learner and an atmosphere of trust in the knowledge that constructive risk-taking can only be of benefit.

Research done in America by Le Ganschow and Richard Sparks and their colleagues propose a Linguistic Coding Differences Hypothesis (LCDH) in support of the following strategies. This hypothesis entails three major findings supported by over ten years of research:

1. Both encoding (producing the language information in written or oral form through writing or speaking) and decoding skills (taking in language information from written or oral sources by listening or reading) in one's native language serve to facilitate learning another language. Weaknesses in any one or several of these skills in one's native language therefore

make foreign language learning more challenging. More specifically, strengths and weaknesses in the linguistic 'codes' of phonology/orthography (sound/symbol relations), syntax (grammar) and semantics (related to meaning of words) all pertain and transfer between languages.

2. The two linguistic areas with the most frequent negative impact on FL learning were, first, phonological-orthographic processing skills, followed by syntactic processing skills. Semantic processing skills were found to be less influential in the Ganschow and Sparks studies (Ganschow *et al.* 1998; Ganschow and Sparks 1995).

3. Negative attitude towards FL learning is more likely a consequence of these identified linguistic processing weaknesses than the initial cause of poor FL performance.

These findings make it clear that reading, writing, listening and speaking skills in the FL are all significantly affected by weaknesses in linguistic coding skills even when the native language has been well mastered through years of developing strategies and overlearning to the point where automaticity has been achieved. The underlying language processing difficulties and differences are still likely to affect the student when exposed to foreign language learning. Even though time constraints are a real factor, techniques and strategies must take into account direct and explicit teaching of linguistic encoding and decoding skills in the foreign language.

To understand the complexity of the linguistic coding differences that affect a dyslexic FL learner, a brief explanation of the major areas of potential weaknesses follow. The reader should keep in mind that any combination of these areas of difficulty can occur within an individual. Also the degree or severity of difficulty varies from individual to individual. For this reason, Ganschow and Sparks suggest picturing dyslexic students in FL classes on a continuum of language processing difficulties. The more areas that are affected and the more severe the difficulties, the more intense the accommodations need to be (Ganschow *et al.* 1995).

A major cause of language processing difficulty lies in struggles with recognising and using language patterns in the new language. Even when dyslexic individuals have good intellectual ability, they may not be able to notice similarities and differences between:

1. print symbols and their related pronunciations (phonological-orthographic processing);

2. grammatical and syntactical structures in the FL compared to their native language (syntactic-grammatical processing);

3. vocabulary and word formation patterns in the FL compared to their native language (semantic processing) (see Gerber 1993; Schneider 1999: Chapter 3).

Dyslexia is predominantly characterised by phonological-orthographic processing problems (e.g. Stanovich and Siegel 1994; Yopp 1992). Without direct and explicit instruction, dyslexic students in an FL class may, for instance, fail to recognise on their own that the German letter pattern 'eu' is pronounced the same way as 'oy' in the native language English. To identify the different syntactic pattern in the 'ne . . . pas' construction in French to express negation compared to the way negatives are formed in English (native language) may seem to be an insurmountable challenge. Likewise, placing the infinitive of the main verb at the end of sentences in German is dissimilar from English language sentence construction and may cause major difficulties. Remembering these constructions and when to use them is often problematic.

Lack of automaticity in native language grammar structures combined with poor working memory will exacerbate the problem, resulting in poorly constructed sentences and often translations with many errors or blanks. A dyslexic student may also not succeed in identifying known word parts inside new vocabulary. An example would be to conclude the meaning of the new German word 'unglaublich' by seeing the prefix 'un', identifying its meaning as a negation, seeing 'glaub' as the root and relating it to the known word 'glauben' (to believe) and then to conclude that 'lich' must be the suffix that identifies the part of speech. Therefore, the new word must mean something in the area of 'not believable' which is precisely its meaning. Such transfer of knowledge would require linguistic analysis skills that need to be taught to dyslexic students explicitly. They cannot be assumed to pick these skills up by mere exposure to the FL and by repeating sentences and phrases.

The authors would additionally like to raise awareness of an area of processing difficulty that has not been researched much at this point – a dyslexic student's ability to identify, understand and use socio-pragmatic language concepts such as idiomatic expressions, humour, jokes, homonyms, homographs, homophones or metaphors in proper discourse in the foreign language. This includes the development of comprehending implicit information 'in between the lines' or spoken or written information (Gerber 1993: 63–103). To be successful in these aspects, phonological-orthographic and grammatical-syntactic skills have to be at a reasonable level of competence. Here, as well, explicit instruction and modelling of learning strategies need to be integrated in the FL classroom to ensure success for the dyslexic learner.

In addition to these areas of linguistic processing difficulties, success in FL learning is often slowed down because of poor short-term and working memory (Gerber 1993: 105–33). Difficulties in storing new information in short-term and working memory as well as in retrieval of information affect all areas of a dyslexic young person's life. Their relevance to FL language learning is apparent as the student tries to commit to memory considerable new vocabulary, new language structures in the areas of phonology, orthography and syntax. When FL information is presented at a 'natural' speed, then the slower speed of retrieval from memory will inevitably require additional instructional support (see principles in Chapter 2) and a slowing down of the speed of presentation for the dyslexic student until such time as the skills become automatic and the language can be presented at its natural pace.

Overall, these descriptions of linguistic processing and information retrieval problems illustrate for the FL educator that while some difficulties in reading, writing, listening and speaking in an FL are normal and to be expected for all FL learners, the dyslexic student is likely to experience much more severe difficulties in all task areas. It therefore is necessary for the FL educator to ensure that the dyslexic student will remain motivated and retain self-esteem during the challenges of learning the FL.

Foreseeing possible difficulties and planning how to avoid them as far as possible can help prevent unnecessary anxiety. The sooner specific strategies are put in place to avoid loss of self-concept through failure, the better for the language learning student. Language learning can and should be fun for all. While making that learning fun can be challenging for the teacher, the spin-off for the student will result in a massive boost in self-esteem and motivation for other subjects as well as the modern language. Finding the right techniques can be a matter of trial and error, and requires the teacher to be aware of a whole range of possible ways of teaching dyslexic young people. Where techniques are in place and these meet with only very limited success, it may be necessary to put accommodations in place to ensure that student is truly being included in the class. This may include accommodations such as giving the dyslexic student a reader who can read material aloud instead of having to read the matter himself or herself. It may mean a scribe who can do the writing part of any lesson. It may mean accepting homework on tape, rather than expecting that work will be written. It is for the teacher to find the accommodation that will enable the student to meet with success. Only through helping the student to achieve success will inclusion truly be happening.

Case studies

The following two case studies serve to demonstrate that for some students, success can be gained. Later chapters will illustrate specifically how FL teachers and their assistants can help alleviate problems and ensure a high degree of success. To retain the anonymity of the students, their names have been changed.

James

James came to me as a child of eight years. He was the second of two children, and had an elder sister who had no difficulties at all in school and enjoyed the whole school experience. James had been assessed as dyslexic in school by the local authority educational psychologist. He came across as a clearly bright boy and the educational psychologist's report supported this hypothesis. James came from a lower middle-class background with supportive parents who were anxious for him to do well. He was a well-motivated but shy boy who made every effort to please his teachers. Discussion with James's mother revealed that she had not suspected any problem until James started to learn to read and write. On reflection, she was able to tell me that James had struggled to learn nursery rhymes and had never really mastered any of them. He had been a little 'uncoordinated' in nursery, but managed to cope with what was asked. When James had been in school for a few months, his mother discovered that James was not learning at the pace of his peers and was rapidly falling behind his classmates. Concerns were at first dismissed by the school who suggested that her expectations were too high, that she was comparing James with his sister and that 'boys were different any way'. For a time James's mother was prepared to accept this, but James started to become withdrawn and clearly unhappy. At this point, the parents took the initiative and insisted on a psychologist's report. By the time the psychologist's report was received, James was in his third year of primary education. James was then allocated extra help in school and the support of a specialist teacher.

Within a short time, James was beginning to make progress. His self-esteem and motivation had returned and his reading skills were developing. James was excelling in art work and his parents were encouraging this at home. Spelling and other writing skills remained poor, but there were signs of progress with James becoming a reasonably logical, but still poor, speller. Structure of work also remained a problem, and when it came time for James to move to secondary school his mother questioned whether it was appropriate to study a foreign language. If he did, which one should he choose? He had a choice of French or German.

I immediately asked how James felt about this himself. He did not want to be different from his peers, and as most of them were going to study French, that was what he wished to do too. Being a little unsure myself at this point, I suggested that he should 'give it a try', but be prepared to work hard at it. James said he would.

After two years, James was enjoying French although he was still not finding it easy. His teachers, however, appreciated his struggles and valued his efforts. Learning and remembering vocabulary were difficult as was the construction of sentences in both speaking and writing. Pronunciation was reasonable, but occasionally James substituted a totally wrong word. Reading was extremely hesitant and every word was thought about before being pronounced. At this stage there was little sign of automaticity in the reading of the passages. However, James pursued his studies for a further two years, and finally gained a Scottish 'O' Grade in French at General level. He was absolutely delighted, as were his teachers, who were aware of the effort and shared in his success.

Melanie

Melanie was a freshmen in an American college at a mid-size, fairly prestigious four-year college in the Midwest. The college admissions programme had given her no other choice but to enter German 111, a fast-paced introductory German course that all students had to take who had taken German before in high school but did not pass the computerised entrance test with a high enough grade to be placed into the second semester course immediately. The course contained 16 students. The general point of view in the FL department was that if one could not pass 100-level introductory FL courses that made up 50 per cent of the two-year FL requirement for the majority of the majors, the student was not 'college material'. Special accommodations were neither publicly advised nor discussed; however, three professors and one adjunct experimented with dyslexia-related accommodations at the time on their own.

Melanie's first quiz results alarmed me immediately. None of the words she wrote were finished. All missed letters at the end, an absolute 'death sentence' for German with all its inflectional and conjugational endings. Many of her letters were indecipherable. Words in sentences were placed in random order without displaying any system to it. The listening comprehension part she did not answer at all.

I decided not to put a grade on the exam nor to give it back to her in class. I needed to talk to her at length in person. Too many errors, and more precisely too many that reminded me of typical dyslexic errors: poor auditory and visual processing skills may have made her fail the listening and reading test; poor visual skills and short-term memory may have kept her from recalling the complete vocabulary words; lack of ability to identify new grammatical language patterns may have let her frantically combine parts of speech without any logic. Lastly, her poor handwriting suggested fine-motor difficulties that are also typical of some dyslexic learners.

A trembling, fearful Melanie appeared for our arranged meeting in my office. Behind closed doors, she admitted that she was afraid to tell me that she had always had difficulties with dictations, text writing and reading in school. She had received speech training as a child, had been in special reading groups in elementary school but then had never really 'qualified' for dyslexia because she had been able to 'beat the system' well up to now. Now she felt stranded because in two weeks of class we had already covered all she had learned in three years of German in high school. She was in an utter state of panic. We went through the exam together and I tested her oral abilities to respond to some information covered in the test. I was amazed how well she was able to perform in this undistracted environment without time pressure, just one-on-one.

I explained and wrote out my observations for her in a chart and kept a box for coping strategies open next to it that she kept filling in during our following meetings. We designed a detailed strategy list which she followed diligently, keeping all her bi-weekly and later once a week meetings with me, as well as her university-paid tutor who initially received suggestions from me to accommodate her. Later, Melanie took over this part. I on my part changed some test tasks that seemed particularly nasty for her and replaced them with others that gave her (and other poorly performing students) a better chance to demonstrate their actual knowledge. To the delight of the entire class, I integrated more kinaesthetic-tactile learning opportunities for all students and directed all of them to practise verbalising their discovery process of language patterns in the areas of grammar, syntax, vocabulary, and even spelling and pronunciation out loud in class. This gave Melanie and everyone else a chance to develop stronger metacognitive thinking skills and self-correction strategies, skills everyone profited from. Melanie and other struggling students, however, benefited from them the most. I also agreed with Melanie never to call on her spontaneously in class but rather to give her a signal to get ready for a response several minutes prior to an expected answer. I offered this accommodation to all students who struggled with this task, often using 'speech vouchers'. Melanie and I remained in constant dialogue about her learning progress, more effective learning strategies for her and teaching strategies for me, and how she could become gradually less dependent on my feedback. Melanie started as a deeply frightened and failing FL student with a grade F. Through her perseverance, the nurturing she received from our increasingly trust-bound interactions and her willingness to take risks with new strategies, she succeeded in the course. She not only received a grade B but also had gained the most solid study strategies that I have ever seen a student develop. A few semesters later she took advantage of completing undergraduate coursework at the school's Luxembourg campus. She lived with a German-speaking family for a year. Her oral performance was excellent after her return although she admitted that her writing skills were still weak.

Success in a foreign language can be achieved

These case studies highlight a number of points for the learning of a foreign language in a school context. Language learning for dyslexic students is unlikely to be easy. Their reading and writing difficulties, as well as associated problems with memory and automaticity of language processing, can be stumbling blocks. With patience, determination on the part of students and tutors, and motivation on the part of the student, success can be achieved. Teachers and those who support the students need to have a repertoire of strategies and techniques to implement for students with dyslexia and other non-identified problems in language learning. This, combined with knowledge and understanding of why it is that students sometimes struggle to learn an FL, helps FL educators and their aides to succeed in maximising the potential of the young people in their charge. FL learning can and should be possible for the vast majority of students. Depending on specific area educational regulations, in some places, only those with most severe difficulties may be considered for an exemption from FL learning or be allowed to take alternative foreign culture courses instead of the FL course. For information on the effectiveness of alternative courses, see Ganschow *et al.* (2000).

It is, however, the right of every student to be able to attempt a foreign language and it is the responsibility of teachers to be aware of how they can maximise students' potential. The only way to find out what that potential may be is to provide the opportunities for success and support students to achieve it.

Chapter 2

Barriers to Foreign Language Learning

Inclusion in a mainstream foreign language classroom can be difficult not only for the dyslexic student, but also for the FL teacher and the FL language assistant and/or special needs assistant or auxiliary. As illustrated in the previous chapter, FL students with dyslexia may be at a disadvantage compared to their non-dyslexic peers because of cognitive and/or accompanying emotional difficulties which may cause language learning to be problematic. While many of these factors may be language-related, not all will be. There are environmental and other barriers to learning which can impact considerably on learning. Affective factors such as attitude, style and means of presentation of the FL educator as well as physical classroom or home study environment can affect the student. Many of these possible problems, however, can be avoided or even eliminated if FL educators and collaborating administrators become aware of them and their negative, detrimental effects. While there are many challenges for the learner with dyslexia, there are also many for the FL educator faced with supporting the student in the classroom and ensuring appropriate strategies and techniques are in place to maximise all students' learning.

The importance of an appropriate FL curriculum cannot be overstated. If the curriculum is geared to the needs of individual FL learners, including those with dyslexia, then students along the entire continuum of FL aptitude stand a good chance of success. How the curriculum is presented is important. The dynamics of the relationship between FL educator and student are an integral part of the success of the teaching programme (for further details, see Chapter 3 on metacognition). Gearing the teaching programme to the needs of the dyslexic FL learner requires a knowledge not just of the curriculum and the young people themselves, but also of more specific linguistic-pedagogical and psychological factors which might affect FL learning. A knowledge and understanding of dyslexia and its associated effects on learning in a general sense can be very helpful. Some of this has been set out in the previous chapter, though it must always be borne in mind that every dyslexic person is an individual and although there may be common factors, no two cases will be identical. Though there are undoubtedly difficulties that will be faced, there will also be areas of strength which can be tapped to aid learning. With this in mind, consideration can be given to facilitating learning and making the experience a positive one for all.

Considerations for choosing a foreign language

There are several aspects for FL educators to consider. For educators, helping dyslexic students and their parents make the best choice regarding an FL experience can cause conflict. Language learning must fit in with the school's subject programme and choice of languages available. Given school and programme constraints, there are various factors to consider (e.g. the number of years which a language should be studied, the languages and teachers available). Possible options such as a stay in the country where the language is spoken so that the language can be encountered in its living form rather than being forced to learn to write and read it in the artificial school environment only, should be taken into account. An introduction to the culture of the country giving priority to basic everyday life tasks of listening, reading and speaking may be more beneficial. Some important considerations are:

- The choice of a foreign language may make an important difference to the degree of success in that language. Depending on the major areas of linguistic processing difficulties (e.g., listening, pronunciation, speaking, grammatical structures, reading and/or writing FL text), some FL languages might be easier to handle than others. Unfortunately, the amount of research data is still small, although there is a considerable volume of anecdotal evidence. References from experienced FL educators who have worked with dyslexic students suggest that students with poor auditory processing skills which manifest in poor listening and speaking skills and who have at least a mediocre sense of sentence structure and of identifying detail in print may experience more success when studying a 'dead' language such as Latin. Those students with poor reading and writing skill, but fairly good listening and pronunciation ability, may best profit from a language that offers a fairly regular transparent letter/sound system. Languages such as Spanish and Italian (and to a lesser extent German) may suit students with poor auditory and visual processing skills as these languages are more similar to English than French in their pronunciation. In languages such as French in which the print version requires more letters in writing than its pronunciation, and the 'silent' parts carry major grammatical information, dyslexic students may find themselves highly challenged.

- Dyslexic students can be extremely creative and innovative in their thought and planning (West 1991), even when they seem quite different from the majority of learners. Where there are stronger visual skills, these can often help compensate for weak phonology and auditory skills. The main challenge lies in finding ways of tapping the skills that do exist into the language learning process. Ways of doing this are discussed later along with the challenges that these present to the FL educator.

- The reason for learning the foreign language needs to be considered. If a young person sees no possibility of ever using the language being taught, motivational factors that might promote learning will instead inhibit learning. If, on the other hand, the student regularly goes on holiday to a particular country, the prospect of being able to communicate in the language of the country is likely to motivate. A child who holidays in France or Israel will be more motivated to learn to speak French or Hebrew than Spanish or German.

- The personalities and teaching styles of the FL educators, along with their willingness to accommodate special needs, are important aspects to consider. Although these aspects are not commonly covered in FL teacher education programmes, they can make a significant difference to students. Those with dyslexia can achieve positive results even with difficult languages such as French or

German when taught in accommodating ways (see Crombie and McColl 2001; Schneider 1999). A potentially very regular and 'easier' language may cause insurmountable difficulties if the FL educator cannot find the appropriate accommodation activities to meet dyslexic students' needs. Many of these activities will be found to be beneficial to many of the students, not just the dyslexic ones. Previous recommendations to teach by the 'natural' or 'communicative' approach (Krashen 1987) which were often unhelpful for dyslexic students are now being replaced by more appropriate, multi-sensory techniques known to be successful.

Principles of accommodations in foreign language teaching

In the inclusive FL classroom it is the responsibility of the teacher to adapt and alter the curriculum for different skill levels. For the dyslexic as well as the gifted student, appropriate accommodations can assure curricular success to some extent. The principles of the following accommodations encompass general good teaching strategies. They are absolute essentials for students with dyslexia, especially when learning a foreign language that exposes them at a relatively fast pace to a completely new language system in sound, print and structure of thoughts (Birsh 1999; Crombie and McColl 2001; Rome and Osman 2002; Schneider 1999). Since these are all areas of potential severe weakness for individuals with dyslexia, FL educators must pay close attention to using the best accommodation strategies within classroom settings. The teacher must therefore adapt, alter and appropriately differentiate the curriculum to make it relevant for dyslexic students. Only then will these students be able to benefit from the additional endeavours of all those involved, including their own. How, then, can a teacher take the necessary steps to enable worthwhile learning to progress?

1. **Multi-sensory techniques**: Multi-sensory techniques actively involve students in using their stronger channels of learning to bring on the weaker ones as they hear, see, say, write trace, act out, and/or move body parts consciously to memorise and retrieve information. Most helpful seem to be kinaesthetic-tactile activities because these activate strong learning channels in dyslexic students. The motto is 'Hear it, see it, say it, write it, act it out' and make learning as active as possible.

2. **Structure**: Restructure the FL language material so that the more complex topic builds on the easier one using explicit explanations and discovery techniques for the students to see how the new information fits in with the previous.

3. **Explicit learning and teaching**: Make language patterns explicit. Whether they are letter–sound related, grammatical, semantic or socio-pragmatic, ensure that the student is in no doubt. Explain to the students if they are unclear. Do not rely on dyslexic students finding the patterns on their own but rather guide these students through thought-provoking questions to 'discover' the new patterns and provide multiple opportunities for the students to verbalise these explicit language patterns.

4. **Overlearning**: Make sure the students receive opportunities for overlearning through a variety of activities. The amount of overlearning necessary to guarantee automaticity in a task depends on the severity of the language processing difficulty in the specific area (e.g. letter/sound, semantics, grammar). It always requires patience on both the teacher's and the learner's side because it is time-consuming and generally requires considerable extra time and commitment.

5. **Metacognition**: Make language learning a 'discovery learning' process in which students turn into 'language detectives'. They should be encouraged to find out:

   • about the structures and uniqueness of the new language

   • why certain expressions are used the way they are

   • how they can self-correct and monitor their own reading and writing.

   This makes all students independent learners. Dyslexic students cannot succeed without this component; the explicit use of mnemonics is helpful (see Chapter 3 on metacognition).

6. **Slowed pace of presentation**: Pace the presentation and learning of new information so that it comes gradually. It should be presented at a slower pace and in logical chunks so that students are able to cope with and comprehend it. They need to practise towards mastery of each concept before the next step of

learning is presented. (Try to teach too much too quickly and the student will become lost.)

7. **Personal motivation**: Engage students by activating their personal strengths and interests and by giving them individual space (e.g. permission to walk around at the back of the room if they become overactive). Do not call on students to spontaneously produce an oral response. Allow them to give a signal that they do not wish to speak. This makes them feel accepted as a whole person and motivated to continue through the difficult parts of FL learning.

8. **Diagnostic and prescriptive factors**: Assess the impact of your teaching on the dyslexic students several times during the lesson. 'Diagnose' the remaining difficulties and teach facing towards them in a direct, explicit way. This will give the students the feeling that their slower processing abilities are being respected.

9. **Short concentration span**: Keep in mind that many dyslexic students burn out losing concentration much faster than non-dyslexic students while focusing on language tasks. The authors' experiences have shown that high-quality concentration in the FL classroom ranges within a five to ten-minute time block for a dyslexic student. If the situation involves traditional explanations of concepts or assignments, and does not involve a concrete kinaesthetic-tactile activity, agree with the dyslexic student on a quick activity that helps recharge concentration. Sometimes this can be achieved by the squeezing of a stress ball or a simple walk around the play area. This lets the FL educator know where the student's level of concentration is at any given time. Another idea is to agree on a gesture the student uses before going to the bathroom for a quick two or three-minute interruption. When quiet reading or written work is done in class, the dyslexic student may profit from simply putting good headphones on to eliminate distracting noise factors coming from the classroom.

(Adapted from Hickey 2000; Rome and Osman 2002. See also Schneider 1999 for an overview of 12–15 different language teaching approaches in the US and Great Britain that use these principles successfully with dyslexic students.)

Regular consultations with the student

Regardless of the FL learner's age, the personal metacognitive kinaesthetic-tactile/hands-on involvement in their own learning is vital to maximise the probabilities of success for memorising and retrieving information in the FL. Important elements which should be taken into account are:

- The student's learning styles in relation to their linguistic weaknesses and strengths due to dyslexia.

- The individual student's linguistic capabilities. Establish which linguistic areas are more or less severely affected and hinder FL learning: phonological, orthographic, semantic, syntactic/ grammatical or socio-pragmatic issues such as idioms, jokes or reading in-between the lines.

- The FL teacher's general teaching style, as well as his or her openness to accommodating students with dyslexia in the classroom. Not all teachers will appreciate the effects that inappropriate or unsuitable teaching styles can impose on dyslexic students. Flexibility is important for all FL teachers, and inclusion of all children in the mainstream FL language classroom means that it is absolutely necessary for teachers to be prepared to adapt to the learning styles of the students. Knowledge of individual pupils' strengths and weaknesses as well as interests (and their specific needs) is essential to ensure that the FL teacher can adapt to meet the requirements of the young people.

- Factors that stimulate personally motivated learning. What motivates the teacher should not be the most important factor. Students all learn in different ways, and it is academic and non-academic motivational factors relating to the learner that can make the world a different place for the dyslexic student. Repeated consultations and discussion with individual pupils and their parents/guardian prior to beginning the FL learning process, and, most importantly, regularly during the learning process are essential. This keeps the FL educator, the pupil and the parents in consistent dialogue about essential personal information that leads beyond sharing frustrations. Topics that should regularly be discussed and re-evaluated are learning styles, the effectiveness of certain study strategies for a variety of home and test assignments. Specific ways of avoiding and alleviating these difficulties are presented later in this book.

- Self-advocacy skills for academic and personal independence. Teach the dyslexic student self-advocacy skills, and provide all parties involved with new ideas or different ways of dealing with difficulties as they occur. The FL educator may keep brief notes on the outcomes of these meetings to help document the social 'learning process' involved for all parties. Regular meetings help build a bond between the student and the FL educator and help keep a positive attitude towards the entire FL learning process. This may be difficult at times because most FL educators chose their profession because they discovered they had a particular gift for foreign languages. Realising that there are students who struggle severely with learning an FL in class despite at least initial motivation may be hard to understand. Through regular conversations about effective study and assessment strategies, supportive in-class activities, possible alternative assignments in and outside of class can be discussed. Through utilising the dyslexic pupils' strengths, a bond of trust can be built where the dyslexic student will feel accepted as a full participant in the FL learning process. This is an essential component for the dyslexic learner to become a successful FL student. Further, by receiving an active role in finding most effective strategies to utilise strengths and to cope with weaknesses in the FL learning context, the dyslexic learner gains self-advocacy skills and confidence.

School ethos

The ethos of the whole school influences learning. When students of all ability levels are given the message that they are valued whatever their contributions, they can then feel safe and at ease to try their best no matter how the ensuing product may turn out. Fear of making a mistake and being mocked can destroy confidence and prevent dyslexic students from attempting to answer at all. Peer group pressure can be a significant factor in dyslexic students' learning progress as well. It is important that the FL teacher diffuse any negative attitude in the peer group by presenting a role model of valuing each individual for the contribution he or she makes in class, even when that contribution is considerably less than that of the rest of the group. Reluctance on the part of a dyslexic pupil to risk making a mistake in the FL classroom is often due to past negative experiences of language learning resulting in inhibited minimal responses both orally and in writing. Confidence building then becomes a major part of the teaching programme, making it even more important to teach in small steps so that the pupil can feel confident that the teacher only expects what has been taught. Attitudes of FL teachers and their assistants can then make the difference between a toe on the ladder of success in language learning or a fall from that same ladder.

Research tells us that the cognitive functioning of dyslexic people is less efficient in the area of language learning than that of non-dyslexic FL learners and that dyslexia is likely to be inherited (Bakker 1990; Gerber 1993). Nevertheless, there is still much that can be done to minimise the effects of heredity and inefficient cognitive language processing. Being prepared to pace the lesson to the individual's learning needs using the principles mentioned in this chapter and considering the strengths and weaknesses of the dyslexic FL learner in a holistic way can make any FL programme accessible to all pupils in the class, not just the ones who find learning easy. Fine-tuning of the learning and teaching programme can be worked on in meetings with the student. The following chapters will investigate just how language learning can be made at least palatable for those with dyslexia, and will explore techniques and strategies that may make language learning motivating and fun for all.

Chapter 3

Metacognition

The terms 'metacognitive strategies' or 'metacognition' mostly occur in educational readings in connection with study strategies. Teachers of dyslexic learners in FL classes must understand these terms and be able to put the strategies into practice on a daily basis. By nature of their disability, those with dyslexia struggle not only with the processing of oral or written language but also with identifying language patterns (e.g., what is the same or different between this conjugated verb and the other?) without explicit instruction about rule patterns (Birsh 1999). Further, dyslexic students struggle with memorisation due to poor short-term or working memory (Birsh 1999). Therefore, engaging dyslexic FL learners actively and explicitly in metacognitive strategies offers compensation strategies for these two weaknesses in particular. It is both rewarding and enjoyable to integrate explicit metacognitive teaching strategies when all students in the inclusive FL classroom, particularly the usually frustrated dyslexic students, experience more joy and success.

What does 'metacognition' mean?

Meta is a Greek prefix and means 'about'. The words 'cognition' or 'cognitive' contain the root *cogni* meaning 'knowing' and 'thinking' or 'knowledge' and 'thought' (Ehrlich 1968). Thus, when educators use 'metacognitive strategies', they raise awareness for strategies among their learners that engage them in direct, explicit thinking processes about (*meta*) thinking (*cognito*) to arrive at knowledge that is available when tasks need to be completed. In other words, metacognitive strategies provide problem-solving strategies. When educators involve their students in thinking about language issues, they involve them in 'metalinguistic thinking', 'linguistic' meaning 'language-related' (Schneider 1999). For any 'metacognitive' or 'metalinguistic' process to be successful, the thinker needs to be in command of the following four skills:

1. They must be aware of the existing problem that needs to be solved.

    (a) *Meta-cognitive*: a flat tyre

    (b) *Meta-linguistic*: a possible spelling error

2. They must be aware of a variety of strategies that could be applied to solve the identified problem.

    (a) *Meta-cognitive*: flat tyre: (a) look for a pump and pump up tyre; (b) borrow pump from someone; (c) go and find a phone and call for help to be picked up; (d) for car: call the Automobile Association; (e) change tyre; (f) hitch-hike to next petrol station; (g) leave car or bike where it is and forget about the incident.

    (b) *Meta-linguistic*: spelling error: (a) ignore sense that word is spelled wrongly; (b) ask teacher how to spell word; (c) ask classmate how to spell word; (d) look word up in dictionary; (e) underline vowels and check what the word that was written actually says and try to find error that way; (f) use spellchecker on computer; (g) continue to write but mark word to go back to it later planning to use either (d), (e) or (f).

3. They must be able to choose the most appropriate of all possible strategies to solve the problem quickly and successfully. The given situation determines the success of the chosen solution to the problem.

    (a) *Meta-cognitive*: Being five minutes from home in bright daylight with a flat tyre makes you choose a different solution from when you are stuck on the road in the middle of the night.

    (b) *Meta-linguistic*: Detecting and fixing a spelling error during a spelling test in school gives you fewer choices than at home where a dictionary, your classnotes, the computer spellchecker and Mum (the living spelling checker) are available.

4. How to assure themselves that an appropriate strategy has been chosen. The problem-solver has to conduct a control procedure after applying a strategy. If the strategy was successful, the problem-solver has completed the task. If not, then another strategy must be selected, applied and tested for effectiveness and procedural steps 2–4 should be repeated until a satisfying solution has been found.

   (a) *Meta-cognitive*: Can I drive the car/bike now without any danger in getting to the destination?

   What is the tyre pressure like? – Test drive.

   (b) *Meta-linguistic*: Am I convinced that the word is spelled correctly now? Do I need more proof from the dictionary, the spellchecker, my own spell checking skills and/or the teacher?

The ability to be able to identify a problem, know about strategies to solve it, apply the most appropriate strategy to solve the problem in a timely manner and double-check the outcome of the applied strategy are the major components of successful metacognitive or metalinguistic skills (Mastropieri and Scruggs 1991; Palincsar and Brown 1987; Yaden and Templeton 1986). Consequently, effective metacognitive and metalinguistic FL language education requires (a) the FL educator to be prepared to model a variety of metalinguistic strategies with self-corrective questioning patterns; (b) the FL educator to be willing to provide sufficient practice time for the students with these strategies; and (c) good observation and copying skills with good questioning techniques for effective self-correction on the part of the FL learner.

What is the FL educator's role in fostering metalinguistic skills?

The FL educator has to (a) model questioning strategies to support self-reflection and self-correction; and (b) provide multiple opportunities for non-threatening practice of metalinguistic strategies in class in a one-to-one tutoring-like setting or in a small group setting. The highly dynamic nature of the inner self-correction dialogue, more or less spoken out loud at least at the semi-vocal level that the FL learner needs to master, requires a consistent dynamic interaction between student and FL educator. For dyslexic students, the question dialogue patterns, gradually to be internalised by the student, need to be overlearned. This can also be established through guided practice between peers which involves alternating role-plays (Bos *et al.* 1989; Schneider and Ganschow 2000). The FL educator needs to consider the following facts for a successful metalinguistic FL teaching/learning experience:

- All students can profit from metalinguistic strategies. Metalinguistic strategies make every learner more independent at a faster pace than without the provision of explicit metalinguistic strategies (Borokowski 1992; Ganschow and Schneider 1997; Mastropieri and Scruggs 1991; Pressley and Woloshyn 1995; Ganschow, Sparks and Schneider 1995).

- For dyslexic students, metalinguistic strategies are lifesavers. Often, dyslexic students are referred to as 'inactive learners' (Deshler *et al.* 1984a, 1984b), because without explicit modelling and over-practice of metalinguistic strategies, dyslexic learners will not be successful students despite personal motivation (Van Kleeck 1994; Wong *et al.* 1986).

- By teaching metalinguistic strategies, the FL educator allows dyslexic students to process the FL language in multi-sensory ways **using their strengths to compensate for auditory and or visual weaknesses.**

- Metalinguistic strategies can be taught along with existing FL textbook structures. The FL educator only has to **analyse the underlying linguistic thinking steps** that lead to a correct response (e.g. gender of compound nouns, case of a noun in word, placement of a verb in an interrogatory sentence). It is these underlying thinking steps that, in general, most FL textbooks and their grammar sections do not make explicit to learners because this does not go along with current overall FL teaching philosophies.

- After these subsequent thinking steps are clear, the FL educator can **design supporting teaching material.** These materials can be used (1) as pre and interim skills assessment tools, (2) as accommodation tools for dyslexic students while taking a test (see Chapter 5 on testing), and (3) for in-class teaching of metalinguistic strategies (see Chapter 4). Highly beneficial are colour and/or shape-coded large card sets that are laminated, as well as laminated sentence strips on which different concepts (vocabulary, grammar, pronunciation, morphology, sentences) are written throughout the school year (for more details on use of these materials, see Chapter 4). The use of water-soluble markers guarantees reusability. While students lay out work or write sentences or words using these cards, they have to verbalise what they are doing and why they are completing a certain linguistic act (e.g. adding a personal ending to a verb or a case ending to a noun or adjective). This way, they engage in FL learning in a multi-sensory way. They are learning in a supportive, structured setting through colour and shape-coding, and are naturally stimulated through the materials to practise metalinguistic processing with their peers and their FL educator. Given the inclusive setting, the FL educator can easily differentiate between difficulty levels by providing good FL learners with uncoloured cards and sentence strips, large laminated poster boards or with more complex tasks using the same card or sentence strip tools. (For further details, see Schneider 1999 and Chapter 4 in this book.)

- The FL educator elicits the students' prior knowledge and arouses interest through **thought-provoking questions and non-verbal gestures.** To ensure success in metalinguistic language processing, the FL educator:

1. Never gives away the answer unless they find out that the students have absolutely no prior knowledge about the concept and could not discover it through thought-provoking questions (e.g. reading a word that is irregular phonically).

2. Elicits students' prior background knowledge on the topic through thought-provoking questions, gestures and the use of multi-sensory structured strategies and materials. Among them could be the colour-coded and shape-coded cards with vocabulary, grammar or pronunciation/spelling information. Toys and other realia can also trigger linguistic key information such as a little mirror reminding the student how

to pronounce the letter H (fogging the mirror), or a little stuffed toy dog reminding them of *cane*, the K-sound in the Italian word for dog or even the entire meaning of *cane*. A gesture associated with the meaning of a particular word, for vocabulary or just a prefix, root or suffix can help remember and recall the information. Even repeatedly used colours for certain grammatical concepts (e.g. gender of a noun, which case a preposition demands) or repeatedly used pictures for certain phrases (e.g. a polite hypothetical expression, a request, an excuse) can help the student retrieve the knowledge through right-brain information access.

3. Leads students to verbalising correct answers through questions. Typical questions would be: 'Why would you write . . . this way?', 'Why would you pronounce it this way?', 'Where would you put this word and why?', 'Can you see a pattern here?', 'How could we memorise it?', 'Tell me what you are thinking.'

4. Explicitly points out that the students have the responsibility and 'ownership' in the discovery process of finding the solution to a given language task (e.g. 'Is there a pattern that helps us remember how to ask a yes/no question versus a question that requires a full sentence answer?', 'Can you detect any logic behind how the compound nouns receive their gender?'). The students turn into 'language detectives' who will need to use many different strategies to find the answer to their 'case'.

5. Uses positive, supportive language to encourage students to continue their metalinguistic 'search process' (e.g. 'great thinking', 'great idea', 'good question', 'What can you do next to get closer to the answer?', 'Who/What could help you?').

6. Provides the students with an opportunity to reiterate the metalinguistic 'working steps' they took to find the correct answer (e.g. 'Tell me again how *you* found the answer.' 'Let's write down what you did to double-check such a structure.').

7. May decide in beginning courses to use the native language for such metalinguistic dialogues to ensure that students, especially the dyslexic ones, feel comfortable with the new

learning processes. Gradually, more and more FL phrases and expressions can be integrated.

- The FL educator provides a **pleasant learning atmosphere** that invites students to focus on finding and correcting reading and writing or speaking errors or to improve their writing composition in style and language. To guarantee a non-threatening, relaxed learning atmosphere in which students feel free to experiment outloud with critical, metalinguistic thinking, the FL educator:

1. Models for students how to find solutions to a task by asking thought-provoking questions, making gestures, and using multi-sensory structured strategies and materials of the kind described above (cards, sentence strips, poster boards, tracing pads, toys, tools).

2. Models for students how to discover a mistake and how to correct it using multi-sensory structured strategies and materials; among them could be strategies such as the finger tapping strategy explained in Chapter 4 to double-check on possible spelling errors (tapping a finger per sound in a syllable of a spelled word), or in text writing to double-check the structure of their paragraphs by colour-coding the written text after completion; another correction device for correct sentence structures would be to re-analyse questionable, especially long sentences with the colour-coding system used initially with the coloured cards that illustrate parts of speech and grammatical functions in a sentence.

3. Allows for 'rethinking time' in class and during test time (e.g. 'Think this over again.', 'Test your answer again.', 'Use your self-correction checklist.').

4. Makes it very clear to students that 'mistakes' are valuable and valued steps of positive learning experiences in this class.

5. Encourages students to ask either each other or the instructor questions (e.g. 'What are you thinking?', 'Why are you saying this/thinking this is the case?').

6. Avoids negative statements or messages at all costs (e.g. 'wrong', 'bad choice', 'thumbs down' or any other non-verbal negative gesture; instead:

(a) Uses positive statements such as 'Good thinking up to here.', 'Interesting thought, tell me more . . . why do you think so?', 'Good thought!', 'What else could we do or think here to explain the situation/remember/understand?'

(b) Provides partial credit for logical thinking behind an error in writing, reading, spelling, pronunciation, speaking or any other task.

- The FL educator provides ample **opportunities to practise** how to recognise important patterns within new information and how to organise them for study purposes. To guarantee most efficient success with pattern recognition, the FL educator:

1. Uses consistent language, phrases and gestures to talk about a new language concept.

2. Lets students discover the 'logic' behind a new language pattern using thought-provoking questions.

3. Uses clear, explicit language and simple sentences.

4. Provides only as much information as the students need to experience discovery of a new pattern based on prior knowledge.

5. Uses well-organised visual support (overheads, blackboard writings).

6. Provides large print hand-outs that allow students to take organised notes and at the same time models for students how to gradually learn to take structured notes for themselves.

7. Provides time in class to organise newly learned information in the appropriate section in the language folder.

8. Provides positive feedback for any signs of organised thinking and metalinguistic reflecting even if answers are not quite correct.

- The FL educator teaches a **variety of mnemonic devices** and encourages students to experiment with them so that they can discover for themselves those strategies that work best. Mnemonic devices help students remember and retrieve information that is difficult to study and recall. They tackle prior knowledge, visualisation skills, sensory learning channels and the idea of the 'unique and surprising', often humorous, to ensure memorisation. To guarantee success with the discovery and application of appropriate mnemonic devices, the teacher:

1. Carefully models the use of mnemonics in different contexts.

2. Explains explicitly why they selected which mnemonic to solve a memorisation skill.

3. Illustrates concretely how different mnemonics can be combined.

4. Encourages students to invent and practise their own designed mnemonic devices.

5 Positively acknowledges students' risk-taking with mnemonic devices.

6. Guides students to find mnemonics that work best for themselves.

What is the student's role in learning metalinguistic skills?

The student also needs to take on specific responsibilities in this dynamic, interactive learning process. The student must:

1. closely observe the teacher's gestures and language;

2. make him/herself ask at least one question per class session, maybe for reassurance ('Did I understand you correctly that . . .?') or because a step is not clear ('Could you please repeat this? You lost me when . . .', 'Why is it that . . .?');

3. practise the observed thinking and problem-solving strategies modelled by the teacher in class and during study time;

4. select for him/herself which study/memorisation or retrieval strategies (mnemonic devices) are best in which situation.

The described metalinguistic dialogue patterns and interactions between FL educator and student and possibly between studying peers are easiest to establish when FL educator and students speak the same mother tongue. In a heterogeneous classroom with several mother tongues and cultures, metalinguistic dialogue just requires more visual clues and gestures supported with consistent simple, clear language to ensure that a simple dialogue about language is possible. In the past, entire heterogeneous FL programmes were built on instruction in the foreign language only, e.g. Natural Approach (Krashen 1987). Using simple, consistently repeated same sentences for explanations supported by colour or shape-coded cards and pictures again and again, while engaging the students physically as much as possible until they understand more and more in and about the FL, sets a useful, interactive framework for metalinguistic language practice with heterogeneous FL learner groups.

What are some mnemonic devices to support metalinguistic skills?

The following mnemonic devices for FL instruction provide examples in German. They may stimulate the reader to discover others in their respective FL. The first author designed and used these examples in her own work with dyslexic students who were learning German as an FL. For further examples to teach mnemonic devices in German as an FL, see Sperber (1989); for English as a native language see Mastropieri and Scruggs (1991); and for Spanish, see. Sparks and Miller (2000). To first enhance metalinguistic skills in the FL, memorisation and information retrieval, the following are successful ideas:

1. sound clues (Table 3.1)

2. letter-shape clues (Table 3.2)

3. crazy stories (Table 3.3)

4. picture clues (Tables 3.4a and b)

5. acronyms (Table 3.5)

6. keywords (Table 3.6)

7. songs and sounds (Table 3.7)

8. gesture and motion clues (Table 3.8)

9. personalisations (Table 3.9).

Table 3.1 Sound clues

DESCRIPTION OF ACTIVITY	EXAMPLE
Sound clues help the memorisation and recall of pronunciation patterns and vocabulary (onomatopoeia)	**Pronunciation** The student links the letter sound with an association in L1* to improve pronunciation. Examples for German: • The letter ß looks like a snake and sounds like a hissing snake. • The letter ü looks like a mouth of a monkey when making the long and short u-sound, like English {oo} in 'boo' or 'book'. **Vocabulary** The student links the letter sound with a cultural-semantic association in L1, e.g. onomatopoeia. '*zischen*' is the action that sounds like what it does when (a) something with fluid disperses under release of a lot of pressure (cork of champagne bottle) (b) something hot touches something cold (a hot pot in a cold, moist sink). Good to combine with the drawing device (Table 3.4a).

*L1 = first language, language of home

Table 3.2 Letter-shape clues

DESCRIPTION OF ACTIVITY	EXAMPLE
Letter clues help memorise and recall spelling patterns (non-phonetic words or word parts) and vocabulary	**Spelling pattern** Linking the letter shape of the letter that causes spelling problems with an association in the L1 or an important keyword that entails it. Example: German word *'Haupt'*. Problem: {p} sounds like {b} when pronounced in word; word means 'main' and 'top part': {p} has rounded letter part at the top, {b} has it at the bottom; further, the words 'top' and 'part' contain {p} as well. Plus, letter {b} is part of 'bottom', the meaning that does *not* match *Haupt*. **Vocabulary** Linking an association in L1 with the shape of a letter that is part of a difficult vocabulary word to remember. Example: German word *Börse*: It refers to 'wallet' and big financial institutions like Wall Street. Letter shape of [ö] reminds studer of coins that are in wallets and found in financial institutions.

Table 3.3 Crazy stories

DESCRIPTION OF ACTIVITY	EXAMPLE
Difficult spelling words (e.g. non-phonetic words) are integrated in groups of up to five in a story that students make up individually. The crazier the story and the shorter, the better for later retrieval. Good to illustrate with picture mnemonics (see Table 3.4a and b)	**German story of eight major vowel teams** *Wir klettern mit Eiern in die Bäume zu den Eulen, während die anderen am See ein riesen Boot mit Saatkorn und Kaugummi füllen.* (We climb with eggs into the trees to the owls while the others are at the lake and fill a big boat with seeds and bubble gum.) **Rare French words in German, ending in suffix –age:** *Garage, Montage, Massage, Stellage, Visage* I went for a 'Massage' (massage) for my 'Visage' (face) in my boyfriend's 'Garage' (garage) where he worked on a 'Montage' (putting together) of his 1963 Chevy Cavalier standing on a high 'Stellage' (scaffolding). Can be all in FL or mixed with L1 depending on what works best for the student.

Table 3.4a Picture clues Part 1

DESCRIPTION OF ACTIVITY	EXAMPLE
Visual illustrations done by student or by teacher help memorise and recall difficult, new vocabulary (see Crazy stories (Table 3.3)), and class activities	**Drawings/pictures/collage including five or six rare, difficult words** Student tells story with these words practising their spelling repeatedly while using them in the story to gain automaticity in correct spelling. (See Crazy stories.)
	Mapping out structures of read texts or content of essays to write in graphic organisers.
	Picture cards that check your spelling: Icon (✋). Use finger-tapping for each sound you heard in each syllable. Icon (✎): Apply syllable division to see if you have all parts in all syllables. Check what you have just written.
	Picture cards that check your reading: Icon (▭). Apply any reading strategies to check if reading made sense. Icon (✎ for ▭): Apply specific syllable division rule for specific word to check if you really understood it.
	When reading a book, the student can attach an overhead transparency over the page and divide difficult words with a water-soluble marker. The marking patterns on the transparency can be used to design a piece of art later. Copy the piece of art, date it and then let students clean transparency for future use.
	Picture card for consonant pronunciation (clipping): Icon (✂)

Table 3.4b Picture clues Part 2

DESCRIPTION OF ACTIVITY	EXAMPLE
Same as in 3.4a	**Linguistic concept: noun gender** Colour-code feminine words in one colour and keep card copies in something that has feminine gender. Do the same in different colours for masculine or neuter words. **Linguistic concept: sentence structure** A train with the parts of a sentence represented by the train carriages. **Letter shapes and pronunciation** Overhead transparency shows goat (in German: *Geiß*) with a lower case 'g' drawn into its face, the g-line leading down through its beard. Student traces the letter first by hand, then with different coloured water-soluble markers, always pronouncing the letter sound while tracing. The goat picture is a keyword for pronunciation and builds vocabulary. **German 'silent R' when preceded by vowel sound /a/** Picture with large lower case 'a' that has swallowed/carries the letter 'r' in words such as *Bar* (bar), *klar* (clear) or *Star* (starling). **Class activity support with picture code cards for better pronunciation** Example: German {ü}-sound poster shows a *Kübel* (bucket) in front of a 'Hütte' (hut) with the two German words each underneath on a card to flip open.

Table 3.5 Acronyms

DESCRIPTION OF ACTIVITY	EXAMPLE
The letters of an entire word each stand for a concept to memorise and recall (e.g. a syllable pattern or study device)	**Note-taking from oral presentation: SLANT** S: Sit up. L: Lean forward. A: Activate your 'thinking machine'. N: Name (verbalise softly) the key information. T: Watch/listen to the speaker carefully for non-verbal and verbal information. **Test-taking: essay question: REMEMBER** R: Read questions carefully. E: Eliminate difficult questions and go for easy ones first. M: Mark keywords in question to focus. E: Eliminate irrelevant information that crosses your mind. M: Mark down keywords – what you want to say. B: Breathe to give brain/thinking machine oxygen. E: Estimate time you can take to answer question. R: Respond and recheck response. **Test-taking: listen and respond in writing: SPENT** S: Sit up. P: Pre-read questions to anticipate topic. E: Eliminate panic thoughts and focus on topic. N: Normalise breathing. T: Trace keywords orally and look for them in print.

Table 3.6 Keywords

DESCRIPTION OF ACTIVITY	EXAMPLE
Keywords that belong to the learners' active vocabulary help retrieve pronunciation of letters, meanings of words or sequences of a grammatical pattern (e.g. statement vs. question). A keyword sentence helps to memorise and recall syllable patterns or learning steps.	**Keyword sentences** **(a) For German syllable patterns** *Komm und sieH die SCHönen Roten und Lila Vögel* Capital letters stand for six types of syllables: Long vowel (L), Short vowel (K), Vowelteam (V), Magic H (H), Schwa (SCH) sound, R-control (R). **(b) For the eight German vowel teams** *Wir klettern mit Eiern in die Bäume zu den Eulen, während die anderen am See ein riesen Boot mit Saatkorn und Kaugummi füllen.* **Pronunciation** Two-syllabic, basic keywords with key sound in initial position, e.g., short A: *Affe* (monkey), long A: *Adler* (eagle). **Vocabulary** A chain of words in alphabetical order, all belonging to a word family (e.g. clothes, furniture) used in game 'I pack my suitcase/moving van and I take …').

Table 3.7 Songs and sounds

DESCRIPTION OF ACTIVITY	EXAMPLE
A melody or entire song helps memorise and recall pronunciation, vocabulary or grammar A sound helps recall specific language patterns (e.g. sentence structure)	**Vocabulary enhancement** with folk song about 'bird wedding' '*Vogelhochzeit*' teaching bird names. **Pronunciation practice** with folk song during which important content words lose letters/sounds as the song progresses from stanza to stanza (e.g., in German: *Mein Hut der hat drei Ecken*) Song works also for practice of verb *haben* in third person singular, a grammatical concept. **Subjunctive practice** with song, '*Ich wünscht ich wär ein Huhn, ich hätt nicht viel zu tut,*' by Comedian Harmonists. **Sentence structure** with a little puppet in a jumping position with a honking horn in hand (or bell) to illustrate 'bracket structure' of main and helping verb in German sentences.

Note: Dyslexic learners seem to have fewer problems with pronunciation and sentence structure if they can learn those concepts in songs than if only exposed to them via print and speaking. (Anecdotal reference, first author)

Table 3.8 Gesture and motion clues

DESCRIPTION OF ACTIVITY	EXAMPLE
A gesture or motion signals meaning or a pronunciation, spellchecker or reading comprehension rule	**Gesture for word meaning or prefix, root or suffix** Meaning of preposition 'against' gestured by hitting fisted knuckles against each other. **Pronunciation** Hand gesture of clipping scissors indicating that speaker/reader must 'clip' additional f-sound added to consonant (e.g. /b +f/ instead of /b/ for letter {B}). **Gesture to remind about spellchecker rule** Finger-tapping technique (tapping one finger per sound in a syllable). **Gestures to remind about Reading Checker rule** Word division strategies to check if a word was read correctly or generally any strategy to check comprehension (e.g. context).

Table 3.9 Personalisations

DESCRIPTION OF ACTIVITY	EXAMPLE
An abstract concept is 'personalised' with characteristics of a human being, animal, flora or fauna	**German single vowels** are always vivacious, and vulnerable; if two or more consonants follow them, they get 'scared' and change their sound from a long to short vowel sound. In English, this happens already when one consonant blocks the vowel. **German consonants** are cool cops. They make sure that the single vowels change their sounds.

The mnemonic devices described should be collected in a **language folder** which students refer to for study purposes. This folder is divided according to topics covered in class with specific sections added for spelling, reading, pronunciation, text writing and vocabulary. The vocabulary section will grow to such an extent that eventually it will require a separate folder. The first author required all students to experiment with such folders, whether dyslexic or not. Not one student complained about the extra work involved in maintaining these language folders. Rather, they all saw the benefits of it and on occasion shared with their teacher how they successfully applied mnemonic devices in social studies, English or maths. The non-dyslexic students could have passed the FL course without these support mechanisms. The dyslexic student, however, would have failed miserably.

It is the dyslexic students in the FL classroom whose survival depends on the FL educator's ability to make room for explicit interactive learning to become proficient in metacognitive thinking and self-correction strategies. Through this reasoning process dyslexic FL learners gain the confidence and knowledge to become an independent successful FL learner. The explicit integration of mnemonic study strategies in the FL curriculum helps in a creative way to memorise and retrieve information that otherwise traditionally was identified as 'There is no reason. Just memorise it.' Each student is invited to use their imagination to invent a story that enhances the memorisation and retrieval process of 'nonsense information'.

In conclusion, it is important to stress once more that in order to integrate the dyslexic student into the inclusive FL class as an active, increasingly independent and successful learner, the FL educator needs to provide an FL learning atmosphere in which language patterns are made explicit through metacognitive dialogues between student and teacher, and among peers. In these dialogues, students practise verbalising their thinking processes and knowledge in the FL regarding pronunciation, grammar, vocabulary, spelling, speaking and writing paradigms, as well as cultural components. They practise thinking out loud, learning from the explicit modelling of the teacher to apply a variety of strategies (a) to identify and solve a language problem (spelling error, reading error, comprehension problem); and (b) to discover the patterns behind a new language concept based on what they have previously learned. All this needs to happen in an error-friendly, language-detective-like atmosphere in which particularly the dyslexic student, who has a weakness in discovering language patterns, gains confidence in succeeding in the FL.

Chapter 4

Foreign Language Learning as a Motivating Successful Experience

Psychology has introduced terminology to educators for two distinct types of motivation: (a) **extrinsic motivation;** and (b) **intrinsic motivation** (Eccles and Wigfield 1985; Pintrich *et al.* 1993). In the context of learning an FL, extrinsic motivation refers to motivation to study and learn that occurs within students which is triggered by stimuli from their environment. Through meaningful rewards or activities students are engaged in such a way that they do not realise that learning is taking place. Intrinsic motivation, on the contrary, refers to motivation to study and learn an FL based on the student's own, personal interests, an inner drive to find out more ·about a particular language, to ask questions, to fulfil assignments and to go beyond these assignments of their own accord to improve foreign language skills and knowledge about the foreign culture. Overall, it is the educational goal to guide students from extrinsic to intrinsic motivation so that they are independently and internally stimulated to continue as lifelong learners in the subject. In FLs more than any other subject, the motto 'if you don't use it, you lose it' applies and makes intrinsic motivation an essential goal.

The question is how to get FL students in inclusive classrooms, including students of all skill levels, background knowledge and linguistic abilities, to become intrinsically motivated and remain engaged with the FL and its culture. With regard to the student with dyslexia, research has discussed whether it is initially lack of motivation to learn an FL and high anxiety about performing poorly that actually cause a dyslexic student to be unsuccessful in FLs (MacIntyre and Gardner 1994a, 1994b; 1995), or whether it is linguistic processing difficulties that eventually cause frustration and loss of motivation. Ganschow, Sparks and their colleagues refer to this explanation in their 'Linguistic Coding Differences Hypothesis' (for an overview of research, see Ganschow *et al.* 1998). In line with this hypothesis, Javorsky *et al.* (1992) provide evidence for the fact that students with dyslexia are as motivated to learn an FL as their peers without such linguistic processing difficulties, even though they struggle significantly with its acquisition.

Further evidence for strong intrinsic motivation to learn an FL is provided in a recent study by Ganschow *et al.* (2000). In this American study, 71 college students with identified learning disabilities were surveyed. They all had been granted an 'FL substitution'. This substitution allowed them to replace actual FL courses required for their majors with courses that provided them with awareness about cultural differences and similarities between a foreign and their own culture (e.g. for Spanish: Spanish History, US Foreign Politics, Spanish Literature in Translation, Hispanic Art). However, 98.1 per cent of the surveyed students indicated they would have preferred to learn the FL itself had it been offered in a modified version that met their disability needs. Further, 83 per cent would have invested extra money and effort to first audit the FL course and then take it for credit if this had been an option at the institution. These responses reflect a high intrinsic motivation to learn an FL despite given linguistic processing difficulties. In addition, these students' transcripts documented determination to succeed in a regular college FL class. Many had attempted to succeed in several FL courses, even several foreign languages to complete the FL requirement for their major before they had to succumb and take the foreign language substitution route in order to graduate in their major.

The fact that motivation does not seem to be the primary obstacle for dyslexics to learn an FL provides interesting suggestions for instruction. First of all, it seems to suggest that teaching of linguistically important content does not have to get lost in 'fake' attempts to entertain and motivate students for the mere sake of producing a 'fun' learning environment. Rather, FL teaching should aim at using specific, linguistically sound preparation and teaching strategies which promise learning success for the individual. The saying 'Nothing succeeds like success' rings true. After all, when students see that they are successful, they are more likely to invest energy in the subject in the future because they received positive feedback for their efforts. Among strategies that are likely to ensure success with dyslexic FL learners, the authors suggest, in accordance with Birsh (1999) and Schneider (1999), the following:

1. **Analyse the content of each unit** in the FL book. FL books generally are organised according to themes such as 'meeting people', 'going shopping', 'taking public transport' or 'writing to a penfriend'. These topics often require a different sequence of presentation of linguistic, grammatical information than might initially be beneficial for dyslexic or otherwise struggling FL students, because more complex structures are often being taught before simple ones. Often structures that are more foreign to the native speaker than another structure are taught earlier in the school year rather than later because they occur with a chosen cultural theme.

2. **Cut each chapter into smaller, logically sequenced units** and focus on teaching explicitly how the new information connects with the previous one. For most students with dyslexia, it is the pace and seemingly illogical sequence of presentation of the material that bring them down (Ganschow *et al.* 2000). There does not seem enough time to explicitly show the students how one topic connects explicitly with the next, what the logical, metalinguistic connection is between the new and the previously learned information. (See Chapter 3 on Metacognition.) Should shifting of linguistic topics from chapter to chapter not be possible, then sufficient time must be taken to explicitly explain to dyslexic students the language patterns involved in the new unit. Otherwise, by nature of their disability, they will *not* be able to pick up these patterns on their own by mere exposure to them through copying them from the board 100 times or being told to learn them by heart. Focus should be given to establishing solid metalinguistic understanding. This is essential for their success.

3. **Structure each lesson carefully.** Introduce the new concept by providing explicit instruction on how the new and the previous

information connect, or provide opportunities for the students to discover this connection themselves successfully by prompting them according to their knowledge base. Break the new concept into small, 'digestible', explicit learning steps with many metalinguistic processing opportunities, and move from one step to the next once you have indication that the students have mastered the previous steps. Move gradually from more guided to less guided activities that are multi-sensory and carefully filtered so that students with dyslexia can achieve success. This requires the careful elimination of unknown information in any practice phase. Provide multiple opportunities for dyslexic students to practise within each learning step to reach automaticity. Keep in mind that students with dyslexia often have a short attention span. Therefore it is beneficial to keep activities of one kind to a 5–10-minute, maximally 15-minute time block. It is beneficial to alternate activities and better to return to an activity again than to stick to one for too long. This may mean having to alternate more frequently than usually between reading, spelling, writing, speaking/listening activities. It may also mean having to structure these alterations more carefully according to which ones build on which, which ones require more complex skills than others, keeping in mind always to move from less complex to more complex tasks.

4. **Teach in a multi-sensory way.** Emphasise learning channels that utilise the dyslexic students' strengths to accommodate their weaknesses often in visual and/or auditory processing. This requires the integration of the kinaesthetic-tactile learning channels predominantly. It means taking advantage of any activities that engage the student through conscious movement of certain body parts, mouth muscles, arm and finger muscles, and the vocal apparatus. Touch is an underused teaching and learning channel that is beneficial to dyslexic learners. When a dyslexic learner cannot memorise a certain linguistic concept or concept differentiation visually or aurally, he or she may be able to do so via the sense of touch-memory and/or muscle-memory. Since many dyslexic students are also coping with some degree of attention deficit disorder, the kinaesthetic-tactile learning engagement will help them focus, catch their attention and increase their ability to remember information. Thus,

multi-sensory instruction will lead to more success and continue to motivate the dyslexic student (and others) intrinsically.

Activities for the foreign language classroom that provide kinaesthetic-tactile learning opportunities include:

(a) the explicit modelling and practising of which mouth and vocal apparatus parts are involved in producing specific sounds (area: pronunciation);

(b) explicit modelling and practising of how to verbalise language concepts while acting them out as persons or sorting colour and/or shape-coded cards on desks or on the floor (areas: sentence structure, vocabulary, spelling, punctuation);

(c) connecting body motions with semantic concepts (areas: prefix, suffix, root meanings for vocabulary enhancement) or sentence/text structure patterns (area: writing);

(d) using different types of fabric and other materials to help with the association and memorisation of different concepts through touch (e.g. soft fabric for voiced letter-sound and hard fabric/material for unvoiced letter-sound);

(e) using mnemonic devices suggested in Chapter 3 for kinaesthetic-tactile learning and teaching tools.

(f) using interactive FL games (areas: vocabulary, pronunciation, speaking grammar).

Further activities that present language in a multi-sensory and fun way are games such as those produced by Miniflashcards Language Games (MLG) Publishing (Thomas *et al.* 1991–2003). These provide for considerable repetition in an attractive, non-threatening way. Skills can be practised and consolidated through games with attractive visual elements (words and picture) elements which complement the auditory and kinaesthetic and aid memory. Different learning styles are readily catered for, and the games and activities can be integrated with the students' daily activities. They not only help build vocabulary, but can be used for grammar practice and story-telling. Taped material can also be used to help pronunciation and intonation, and cards can be customised for use with the Drake Language Master. Further information on the Language Master is in Chapter 6.

5. **Teach in a metacognitive/metalinguistic way.** Particularly for students with dyslexia, it is essential to provide ample opportunities to process language concepts explicitly. This can be achieved through verbalising certain language patterns regarding pronunciation and spelling, sentence structure, vocabulary formation, grammatical word formation (e.g. tense) and why they need to be there. Specific teacher–student interactions and the use of mnemonic devices to enhance instrinsic motivation and success have been described in Chapter 3.

6. **Provide opportunities for overlearning.** Provide enough repetition of each individual learning step so that automaticity can be reached. This can be achieved by providing a variety of multi-sensory structured activities and does not have to be boring because one activity is being repeated. Such repetition should also be avoided because it leads to blind memorisation of how to complete a task without achieving its purpose of providing practice for thorough processing and understanding of a concept. Providing opportunities for overlearning through practising a concept in a variety of contexts and tasks is the goal. For instance, regular paper–pencil tasks can be preceded by a variety of more to less guided practice forms using coloured cards and markers, the blackboard, picture-to-text matching activities, gradually moving from larger print to smaller print; moving from coloured print to black and white print on cards; moving from card sorting tasks to paper–pencil tasks; moving from more receptive to more productive tasks (e.g. first viewing and listening and then viewing and briefly responding in written form to responding orally only).

With regard to paper-pencil tasks, the FL educator needs to be aware of a crucial fact: dyslexic students generally cannot rely on successful transfer of mental ideas and concepts onto the paper. **Spelling and sentence structure** concepts that dyslexic students may have understood correctly, in theory, often appear on paper jumbled and incorrect. Also word memorisation and retrieval are a problem because of frequent poor short-term memory skills and/or visual/auditory memory problems to various degrees. Errors in these areas usually cannot be blamed on lack of trying, concentration or focus. Word selection, spelling and sentence structure errors occur in numbers often too massive to correct. These students need to over-practise their muscle-memory in arms, fingers and handwriting techniques through a variety of interactive pair work, small group or individual activities to become successful.

Memorising and retrieving vocabulary with its gender specifics is common to many foreign languages. Each word that belongs to a different part of speech may therefore receive a different colour. Gender differences among nouns can be identified through colours within the same colour family of the noun (e.g. different shades of green). Most recent vocabulary words are kept on colour-coded cards on a key ring for easy access to review visually and aurally in school and at home. Well-remembered cards can be organised in a shoebox according to degree of security of the memorisation. A check sheet in the front of the box keeps track of dates when the words where reviewed and correctly/incorrectly memorised (indicated by a + sign or - sign). Five consecutive + signs make the vocabulary word move into the first category of the box. Ten consecutive + signs place the card into the second category and so forth. This type of filing system allows students to play a variety of vocabulary-strengthening language games alone or in pairs. The teacher can designate a certain amount of time each class period for student-initiated vocabulary review which integrates the use of the key ring and/or the vocabulary box. All students in the inclusive classroom are integrated into this activity, each one at his or her level of comfort. Points are given towards a reward for highest effort in practising vocabulary. Each class can design game rules independently.

To reach automaticity in correct **spelling**, especially of words that do not follow any spelling patterns, massive letter sequence tracing and simultaneous pronunciation of each letter are necessary. For words that cannot be sounded out, the student traces the letters and pronounces their letter names (the sound the letter makes when said in the alphabet) along with each traced letter. At the end of the word, the student blends the word together into what it really sounds like and signals this process by sliding the finger along underneath the traced letters. Phonetic words, words that can be sounded out, receive a slightly different 'treatment' for overlearning. Here, the student traces each letter of the word again but this time pronounces a sound (not the letter name) for each letter pattern. Again the student blends all sounds together and signals this process kinaesthetically by sliding the finger along underneath the traced letters. For such tracing activities, one can use the bare table or desk top, a piece of soft carpet that makes the traced letters visible, or a tray filled with sand, rice or millet. Writing such words in the designated colour of their part of speech and their gender-specificity on paper offers another retrieval option when in doubt how to spell a word or in which place in the sentence to use it. If, for instance, a student of German cannot remember whether a specific word in a sentence needs to be capitalised but remembers that he or she practised saying and writing the word in the 'noun colour', the student will confidently capitalise the word since he or she knows that all nouns in German need to be capitalised at all times. To enhance gender-specific knowledge of nouns either being feminine, neuter or masculine, noun cards in their designated colours can be kept in items that are described as nouns in either of these genders (e.g. keep all masculine German nouns in the fridge in a stack because in German 'fridge' is masculine). (See also Schneider 1999.)

To make over-practising **pronunciation and correct spelling** meaningful and personally engaging from the beginning, students must receive explicit clear instruction on how to move specific mouth parts to produce the foreign language sounds correctly. Creative, humorous links to the native language, in fact any mnemonic devices that the teacher or the students themselves can invent to make pronunciation easier, are welcome. The more the students are actively involved in explicitly finding ways to produce the correct sounds to the corresponding spelling patterns, the more motivated and successful they will be. This is usually a part in FL instruction that is left up to independent work in language laboratories. Listening to audio tapes, however, can be a most frustrating nightmare for dyslexic students with poor auditory and/or visual processing skills (Ganschow *et al.* 2000). Providing all students with concrete visual, kinaesthetic-tactile cues as to how to produce certain sounds and how to spell them in the FL in class is a much faster and more effective way to reach success in reading, pronunciation, speaking and spelling tasks than leaving it up to computer and/or language laboratory assignments only.

Devoting 5–10 minutes for the first few weeks in introductory FL courses to explicit sound-letter instruction in class where students can watch themselves and each other in mirrors producing sounds, feeling what their vocal cords and other voice box parts do to come closer and closer to good foreign pronunciation, is worth the effort. Students can keep track of their own discoveries and mnemonic devices on letter-sound pattern overview sheets which they keep available for personal reference. These sheets can contain categories for (1) a specific letter pattern; (2) what to do to pronounce it; (3) how to remember to pronounce it correctly; (4) keywords that help trigger the pronunciation in the FL; and (5) other spellings with the same pronunciation. Meaningful follow-up activities to keep practising pronunciation in relation to print representation can be practised by reading easy, short narrative and poetry texts in the FL. The student is guided to focus on specific letter-sound patterns that seem to cause him or her difficulties, working on no more than three to five at a time. When the student feels ready, he or she can record the reading passage on tape and receive feedback from the instructor regarding specific aspects previously agreed upon. Such tasks give each student the chance to work at his or her own pace, focus on individual strengths and/or weaknesses and receive opportunities to improve pronunciation skills over time. Through such tasks, the nightmare situation for dyslexic students to be called on the spot to respond in comprehensible FL phrases or sentences is removed. As motivated students, those with dyslexia can fine-tune their skills while learning a lot about letter-sound patterns in the words of the FL when practising with multiple authentic literature samples.

To improve spelling skills in the FL for dyslexic learners (and others), it helps to provide students with concrete '**finger-tapping**' strategies to assist them in self-monitoring their spelling productions. In alphabetic languages finger-tapping refers to the kinaesthetic-tactile strategy of tapping a finger down on the desk or sheet of paper for each sound in a syllable with the non-writing hand. A word with more than one syllable is tapped syllable by syllable so that one never runs out of fingers on the tapping hand for sounds in a syllable. For instance, the FL (German) word '*Rasen*' (meadow) has two syllables. The student taps the first syllable '*Ra*' with the thumb and the forefinger saying each sound and then writes the corresponding letter pattern down. For the second syllable '*sen*', the student repeats the procedure tapping three fingers down for three different sounds. The student reads back to himself or herself what he or she sees written on paper (not what he or she remembers) to double-check if all parts of the word are there and spelled correctly. This finger-tapping procedure is extremely helpful when more complex words need to be spelled. Initially, the FL educator must provide time to model the procedure and let the students practise enough to use it independently. Trained tutors and helpers can provide additional support.

Dyslexic students can also become successful in using correct **sentence structures and grammatical word structures** (e.g. verb conjugations, adjective or noun declinations) by repeatedly practising and memorising a strict colour-coding system to simplify the retrieval of different sentence patterns and grammatical word patterns. For sentence structure patterns, each part of speech in a specific role in the sentence receives a specific colour which the student learns by heart by building hundreds of sentences with this pattern using his or her own set of laminated colour-coded cards on which different words for different sentences are written for repeated practice. As the sentences become more complex, so do the number of colour-coded sentence cards for a sentence. The ultimate knowledge test occurs when the student starts building sentences on white laminated cards relying on internalised colour-coding mnemonics. The teacher introduces new sentence grammar concepts explicitly by using the same colour-coding system for each grammatical 'job' in the sentence and having the students initially practise with these same colour-coded cards in class in groups, verbalising the metalinguistic reasoning behind the newly learned grammatical concept and how it fits in with already learned information. For grammatical word patterns, case endings match those colours they refer to in the sentence (e.g. direct object is light blue -> ending for adjective and noun is light blue as well). Verb endings take the colour of their referring noun (verb–noun congruence). Multiple indicators that identify a specific verb tense in auxiliary and main verb are identified with the same colour-code or shape-code if the number of colours becomes too confusing for the teacher or the students. The card materials offer a great variety of practice opportunities for which students can be grouped depending on their linguistic comfort zones so that all students are engaged in learning at their pace. The sentence materials and practice modes varying from bigger cards to smaller cards to be worked with on desks, on the floor or on pocket charts. Sentence writing can be practised on large laminated colour strips or progressing onto white strips or simple paper.

Dyslexic students can also become successful in producing logical sequences of narrative and expository **text structures with organised kinaesthetic-tactile learning.** For texts, the basic paragraph features are given colour codes. Initially, paper outlines are written in keywords on laminated colour-coded key-shaped cards to connect key ideas with keywords. The cards are big enough to change these keywords into entire sentences later. The topic sentence with the main idea of the paragraph is green, each supporting detail, fact or reason (note that there can be more than one) is written on a yellow key card, immediately followed by one or several red keys that contain the examples that support each detail. When students are ready to write several paragraph texts, each yellow card information becomes the topic sentence of each new paragraph. Little blue key cards are used to provide logical conjunction words such as 'then', 'consequently' or 'however' once the students have learned these in the FL. The green sentence is taken as the overall topic sentence of the introductory paragraph of the paper. This green sentence is supported by the overall outline of the paper listing the different yellow card topics. The final paragraph of the paper repeats the content of the initial green key sentence only in a slightly different way (adapted from Auman 2002).

Dyslexic students enjoy explicitly constructing papers with such concrete 'scaffolding material' at hand. Students with dyslexia (and others) lose the fear of writing when given such concrete 'architectural tools' to produce text. First, students can practise in class constructing texts together in teams, checking on each other's sentence structure and spelling only after the overall content of the text is agreed upon. Students can move key cards, rewrite key cards, practise social interaction and metalinguistic thinking by discussing what needs to be done and why. Finally they can be proud of the end product of a cohesive little text in the FL which they can illustrate in their own way whether they work in teams or alone. This colour-coding system can also be used to form structural cues for retelling information in the FL, either the story the student wrote or another one that is outlined on the coloured keys. Gradually using less and less of the visual, kinaesthetic-tactile cues, the student learns to speak increasingly more freely in more cohesive and complex ways.

7. **Teach all linguistic concepts explicitly.** Students with dyslexia will not be able to understand and properly use FL patterns orally or in writing without explicit explanation. Therefore, there are essential components of language that must be taught explicitly. Among these are:

   (a) letter-sound relationships for proper pronunciation, reading and spelling (e.g. which sound requires which spelling and vice versa);

   (b) common vocabulary patterns of compounds, prefix-root and suffix patterns for proper reading and listening comprehension, writing and spelling;

   (c) grammatical concepts for proper reading and listening comprehension, writing, speaking and spelling;

   (d) socio-pragmatic information about the FL such as idiomatic expressions, typical non-verbal gestures in specific social settings (e.g. invitations, greeting people of different ages and education) to ensure successful experiences in understanding and sending proper socio-cultural cues in verbal, non-verbal or written contexts.

   In short, the FL educator cannot assume that the dyslexic students will acquire any knowledge of language patterns implicitly on their own due to their disability despite average to above-average intelligence. All teaching and learning strategies suggested in this chapter and Chapter 3 contain the characteristic of being explicit and thus provide examples for explicit instruction.

At the end of this chapter, the reader may think that all these suggested strategies are in essence good teaching skills in general. We, the authors, agree wholeheartedly. However, for the student with dyslexia, the careful, explicit consideration and application of these skills are essential for a successful FL learning experience and for a more enthusiastic, motivated learner in your classroom (see also Hill *et al.* 1995; Kenneweg 1988; Schneider 1999; Sparks and Miller 2000).

Chapter 5

Preparing for and Passing Tests

Implications of dyslexia for students working towards exams

Like any other student, the student with dyslexia has to prepare, take and pass tests in foreign language classes to be successful. This often causes insurmountable difficulties for dyslexic students because both regular FL test-taking conditions as well as certain tasks almost guarantee failure. The following statements are taken from the Ganschow, Philips and Schneider (2000) study in which dyslexic students told of their frustrating experiences in unmodified college FL courses. They illustrate the high amount of motivation and effort that dyslexic students put into course and test preparations without receiving positive rewards through successful grades. One student, for example, noted, 'I tried 175 percent to just receive a D or F' (p. 119). Another dyslexic student pointed out that he knew he was 'unable to control the problem … [and] truly could not master the language even after living in it for two months' (p. 120). Yet another testified that even after four years of high school Spanish she still could not pass the beginning level college FL course (p. 118). She also agreed with her peer who identified the FL courses as 'too fast for my level of learning' (p. 120).

The above statements give clear indications for FL educators who have dyslexic students in their classes. To make successful test results a realistic option for them, four areas need to be addressed:

1. explicit instruction of test preparation strategies

2. explicit instruction of test-taking strategies

3. careful selection of test tasks

4. appropriate test-taking modifications.

At first, accommodations regarding the preparation and completion of foreign language tests are considered. These include the following suggestions.

Explicit instruction of test preparation strategies

In an inclusive classroom, *all* students will benefit from explicit test preparation instruction. The dyslexic student, however, will benefit most from these strategies, because without this specific support he or she is doomed to fail. Initially, the FL educator can motivate students to personally **experiment with different test preparation strategies**. Students need to learn to **evaluate which strategy works best** for them for which test task. This involves learning to keep a record of the number and length of times they practised a certain strategy prior to a test. They also record over time which strategy helped them best for which kind of test task. This can be cross-checked with parents if desired. To encourage this self-monitoring, the FL educator may provide the following incentive: the more a student practises with a variety of test preparation strategies, the more 'study points' he or she can receive that will count towards the final FL grade or even specifically towards decreasing/alleviating errors in the actual examination. Examples of test preparation strategies that should be taught explicitly are the following.

Mnemonic devices

Since ancient times, mnemonic devices have been an effective memorisation tool for people of all ages. They have allowed actors, politicians and students to retrieve large portions of information successfully (Sperber 1989). For all FL areas, namely grammar, syntax, vocabulary, culture, pragmatics, phonology and/or orthography, any of the mnemonic strategies suggested in Chapter 3 promise success. It must be kept in mind, however, that the dyslexic

FL student depends on explicit introduction to and multiple practice with these mnemonic devices, applying the 'talk-out-loud metacognitive processing strategies' to have them available as useful tools in test-taking situations. For examples, see Chapter 3 (specifically Tables 3.1–3.9).

Multi-sensory, structured studying

Further, the FL educator should model and encourage memorising FL information by using as many learning channels simultaneously as possible, especially the kinaesthetic-tactile (touch-motion) learning channels (Birsh 1999; Schneider 1999). For the memorisation of vocabulary, proper pronunciation or general cultural, pragmatic or grammatical/syntactic information, multi-sensory structured studying may include **talking out loud** while reading or taking notes, talking out loud while writing study scripts or while spelling new vocabulary, talking out loud while writing sentences or paragraphs, or while outlining information. It can also include the use of a **tape recorder**. The student can record vocabulary in the foreign and/or the native language and then respond to each word with the corresponding translation in the other language on tape and/or in writing.

If the student's pronunciation in the FL is poor, a peer or the FL educator can record the FL vocabulary of each chapter on a tape, leaving enough time for the student's response. This response may include a repetition of the FL word and then be followed by its translation. From personal experience, the first author can attest that this support at most takes 20 minutes per regular FL vocabulary chapter. The multi-sensory structured studying of specific grammatical and syntactical FL information may include the use of a personal set of laminated **colour-coded** and/or **white cards** to review and practise grammatical and syntactical concepts learned in class. This would be especially important and helpful (a) if the same type of cards were used in introducing FL students to the grammatical/syntactic concepts initially in class; and (b) if the use of empty/clear colour-coded or white cards were allowed as an accommodation device during the exam (see section on Appropriate test-taking modifications later in this chapter). The cards then contain parts of speech necessary to form coherent and cohesive sentences (e.g. nouns, verbs, adjectives, adverbs, conjunctions, connectives, articles). These parts of speech are colour-coded according to their syntactic role in the sentence. Thus, all verbs and verb parts that participate in forming predicates are one colour or remain in one family of colour ranging from light to dark (e.g. light to dark red).

All nouns and adjectives and articles in the role of a direct object are one particular colour (e.g. blue), and those that signify an indirect object are another distinctly different colour (e.g. green). For the review of any multi-syllabic vocabulary, colour-coded and white cards can benefit the student while reviewing systematically and in a multi-sensory way the semantic chunking of vocabulary knowledge. These cards would signify known compounds or prefixes, roots or suffixes initially by colour and then later just by being placed on a separate white card. An opportunity to see and sort the word parts (morphemes) according to known and possibly unknown components supports vocabulary learning through semantic chunking and assists students in realising the efficiency of 'vocabulary transfer' of known information. It prevents the dyslexic FL learner (and any other FL learner) from naturally overloading the brain with unnecessary whole-word vocabulary memorisation after a base vocabulary in the FL has been established. For instance, when the FL is Latin or a spoken Romance language (e.g. Italian, French, or Spanish), modelling the use of and providing comparative FL exercises with a special **dictionary that explains the meanings of common prefixes, roots and suffixes** may be most beneficial in speeding up the process of independent vocabulary acquisition. This type of dictionary explains the meanings of Latin and Greek-based prefixes, roots and suffixes, providing examples and activities for practice in English. (For an English language-based dictionary, see Ehrlich 1968.) Knowledge of the meanings of at least the most common prefixes, roots and suffixes enables dyslexic students (and others) explicitly to identify the meaning of potentially unfamiliar FL words by analysing the meaning of its prefix, root and suffix parts. For instance, if the student knows that the suffix '-or' indicates a profession, the root 'scrip/script/scrit' or 'scriv' refers to the action of writing, and that the prefix 'e-' means 'out', the student can infer that in Spanish an *escritor* is a writer, a person who writes 'out' information or thoughts; that in Italian *scrittore* is a writer; and in French an *écrivain* is a writer.

Dyslexic students have to be shown explicitly how to transfer the English suffix '-or' to the Spanish suffix '-or', the Italian suffix '-ore' or the French suffix '-ain', all carrying the same meaning. By nature of their disability, dyslexic students also need to be made explicitly aware of the fact that the root in the English and the FL word are the same (with slight variation). Often, they will not detect it on their own before they have been taught explicitly how to look for these study strategies. Once shown and practised, however, they will gladly use these tools and enjoy being as successful as their peers who did not necessarily need this initial explicit instruction to be successful. In addition to such **prefix, suffix, root awareness** training with cards, dyslexic students will profit from using cards to develop **semantic word families** in which either the root of the word, the prefix or the suffix is the same. For instance, they would build words with their cards in class and at home for practice and then write them down with the translation based on using prefix, root, suffix, or compound word knowledge for the FL educator to check and provide study points for. A semantic word family around the Italian suffix -ZIONE (English -tion, meaning turning verb in root into noun) could include the following words: dis-simul-a-zione (dissimulation); at-ten-zion (attention), con-tamin-a-zione (contamination). It may be helpful to first introduce these vocabulary and grammar card exercises with English examples using the English language to ensure that students realise the study steps and their transfer value into the FL.

Summary information charts

The FL educator can insist on collecting this structured explicit study information separately on **summary information charts.** Pronunciation and spelling information is summarised on sound/letter information charts. Grammatical information can be collected on grammar summary charts. Semantic/vocabulary information compiled in simple and personalised ways (e.g. colour-coding pictures), enriched with pragmatic contextual clues, if appropriate, and personalised by other individualised study clues such as specific keywords and mnemonic devices that appeal to the individual learner in an especially effective way can be put on semantic information charts. A summary chart for pronunciation and/or spelling may include the categories:

1. TOPIC

2. RULE in my words

3. WAYS TO REMEMBER (mnemonic device that works for me, even if I use my native language)

4. EXAMPLES (can be funny and include illustration)

5. ANYTHING ELSE that helps me remember.

A summary chart for grammar/syntax information may include the same categories only specifying the colour-coding used in class under EXAMPLES. For vocabulary charts the same basic categories can be used as well. Depending on the type of vocabulary summary, however, it might be more efficient to use word family summary charts that remind the student of the generalisability of vocabulary knowledge. This chart represents a graphic organiser. Word family charts first highlight the part of the word under which the family is gathered (prefix, root, suffix or compound) and indicate its meaning (e.g. Root: 'scrib/script/scri/scriv' = to write). Then, three separate lines across for one prefix, one root and one suffix each gives structure room to fill in a new FL word. A fourth, longer line provides room to write the entire FL word down and a fifth line provides space to write the translation in the native language down (e.g. French: *é-criv-ain* = '*écrivain*' = writer). One uninterrupted line underneath these five lines allows the student to write a sample sentence using the new word in context (e.g. *Je ne suis pas un écrivain beau* = I am not a good writer). Downwards these two types of rows are repeated for more examples in the chosen word family pattern.

When idiomatic phrases and expressions and cultural information are introduced, separate summary sheets may be useful to ensure that these valuable, usually very difficult 'implicit' and non-concrete issues regarding the FL language and its culture are explicitly summarised in an organised fashion easily retrievable for the dyslexic student. Such summary sheets may include categories such as (a) EXPRESSION; (b) MEANING AND CULTURAL CONTEXT; (c) COMPARABLE EXPRESSION IN MY LANGUAGE; (d) WAYS TO REMEMBER IT (illustration, direct translation); (e) EXAMPLE; and (f) ANYTHING ELSE?

Again, due to the nature of the disability, dyslexic students need to be shown how to make and utilise such study material through explicit instruction. Once shown and provided with practice opportunity, they will gladly and successfully apply these strategies. Without this explicit instruction, however, they will fail to do so and remain unsuccessful.

'Mock' exams

Preparation for oral exams may include providing **'mock' oral exams** for students in pairs or individually with the FL educator, as well as regular voluntary **five-minute one-on-one meetings** with the FL educator in the office for mere practice purposes. The FL educator can give the often shy and quiet dyslexic student, scared of being called on spontaneously in the classroom, the opportunity to practise free of peer pressure in this situation. This option should be open to all students. Experience has shown that only a few students take advantage of this opportunity. So the FL instructor does not need to worry about overextending his or her time with this offer. Students can sign up for a limited number of discussion spots each week and may receive extra points for participation. Further, the FL instructor can provide some **practice questions** which the student can **prepare with peers or alone** ahead of time with written cue words and/or pictures as guidelines and then with decreasing visual support practise speaking responses on tape or giving them to each other in pairs.

Time management and task organisation

Since dyslexic students characteristically struggle with time management and task organisation, explicit instructions on keeping a record of exam preparation time, types of strategies used and self-observations of their effect are essential. This will lead the dyslexic FL student to become an independent FL learner with good self-regulation and self-advocacy skills, skills that good FL learners usually possess without explicit instruction (*Perspectives*, Winter 2003). Recording charts may include the identified categories.

Depending on the students' ages and their individually differing degree of language processing difficulties, rewards may be interspersed sooner or later in the recording process and increase in challenges over time. For instance, at the beginning a reward that is meaningful to the student may be provided after keeping track of study times for one week. The next reward is not provided until the student has kept proper track of his or her study time *and* types of strategies used for two weeks. More challenging yet would be to receive a reward only after having kept track over a period of three weeks of study time, study strategies and their effect, using models that the teacher set or checking off some phrases that are provided on the record chart. Examples of such choices to check off would be:

Vocabulary

(a) I could remember the word using the mnemonic device not at all/well/very well.

(b) I could recall the expression visualising the picture on the summary chart not at all/well/very well.

Spelling

(a) I spelled the word correctly/almost correctly/not at all correctly applying the non-phonetic memorisation strategy.

(b) I spelled the word correctly/almost correctly/using the doubling rule.

Syntax

(a) I wrote the sentence correctly/almost correctly/using the multi-coloured cards.

(b) I wrote the sentence correctly/almost correctly/using the white cards.

Grammar

(a) I wrote the verb ending correctly/almost correctly using the mnemonic device for the verb/noun agreement.

(b) I wrote the adjective and noun ending correctly/almost correctly using the mnemonic device for it and the colour coding.

For the student and his or her FL educators to see progress measured over time, each report form has to contain the appropriate date. The older the student, the more likely it is that this information can be gathered on a graphics computer program (e.g. Microsoft Word, Excel) and be charted.

Explicit instruction of test-taking strategies

Even though in an inclusive classroom *all* students will benefit from explicit test-taking strategies, it is the dyslexic student who will depend on these most for success. Many helpful books have been published on the topic of test-taking strategies (e.g. Brown 2000; Deshler *et al.* 1984a, 1984b; Ellis 2000) but none specific to FL learning and its special challenges for students with languag_ processing difficulties such as dyslexia.

The survival FL test-taking kit

The following materials should be required basic test-taking tools:

- highlighters in each of the colours needed to be able to analyse the parts of speech and their syntactic roles in a sentence;

- coloured markers or highlighters to identify known parts of vocabulary words (compounds, prefixes, roots or suffixes) as concrete multi-sensory tools to retrieve knowledge in case of panic;

- plain pieces of scrap paper to experiment with thoughts and spellings, to brainstorm or retrieve mnemonic devices;

- several sharpened pencils;

- a stress ball to release mounting tension and anxiety;

- a watch with a large face to make time management easier.

Permission to ask the examiner questions

Further, it helps when the FL educator explains at the beginning of each test that students can come and ask questions if they do not understand a test task. It must be made clear to the students that the examiner will not give the student the answer but rather, much like using the metalinguistic questioning strategies, will respond with a prompting question in return that will help the student get on the right thinking/problem-solving track. An open, learner-friendly test atmosphere is essential for bringing out best grades among all students in an inclusive FL classroom. It is almost a survival issue for the characteristically highly anxious dyslexic FL learner.

Initial evaluation of difficulty level of test

Initially, the FL educator models and provides practice for the dyslexic student on how to analyse the test tasks instead of randomly in a panicky fashion rushing to answer questions that he or she might not even have processed thoroughly enough to answer correctly. First, the student must take time to find out if he or she really understands each task. Then, using a plus sign for 'easy' tasks, a minus sign for 'difficult' tasks, a question mark for a task that is unclear to the student, and a wiggly line for a task in-between easy and difficult provides the student with landmarks for sequencing through completing the test in an efficient way. Students with a high level of anxiety may be best to start with the easiest task, working towards the harder ones to avoid anxiety blocking the thinking process from the start. Students who know that their concentration fades quickly may want to begin with a more challenging task and leave the easier ones for later.

Semi-vocalising

The dyslexic student should also be encouraged to semi-vocalise his or her thinking during the test to keep focused and ready to catch processing mistakes with this strategy. This, of course, needs to occur in a distraction-free, separate test space to avoid distracting other students.

Explicit matching of effective strategy with test task

It is the FL educator's responsibility to make explicit which strategies might be most beneficial for which test task by modelling them and then providing ample practice opportunities in class and through homework assignments. Here, computer-generated test simulations that score the results for student and teacher to review may be a useful tool because students can practise on their own time and at their own pace. Contributions from students regarding test-taking strategies should be encouraged and integrated in practice time to teach the dyslexic student:

- that learning through trial and error is a positive process for all learners;

- that, based on evidence, strategies can be revised, remodelled and accommodated so that they will fulfil the initial purpose;

- that becoming an actively involved FL learner is a positive, rewarding experience.

Overall, once the FL educator has identified the types of test task that will appear in the forthcoming examination, he or she may wish to provide explicit preparation strategies specific to the forthcoming test task. Further, the following test-taking suggestions address specific, commonly used FL test tasks.

Multiple choice or matching tasks

The strategy of first 'eliminating what it is definitely *not*' may work best for dyslexic students. In a metalinguistic dialogue with the students (see Chapter 3), the FL educator can model for them how to look for keywords to identify the correct responses in such types of tasks.

Short sentence or small paragraph responses

The FL educator models in class how students can implement text organisation strategies (for details, see text writing strategies at the end of Chapter 4) in the actual test situation. Students use colour markers to identify essential parts of sentences and text parts just as practised previously in class and during homework assignments with coloured and white cards to ensure complete sentences and/or cohesive paragraphs.

Gap-filling tasks (cloze procedure)

When gap-filling tasks are used, choices should be provided below or above the gap to give the dyslexic student at least some chance of success with this type of task. To avoid complete guessing, the FL educator must spend ample time engaging the dyslexic student in thought-provoking metalinguistic dialogues. (See Chapter 3). This process makes the student confident and at least semi-successful because he or she knows the types and sequences of thinking steps that must be used to find the correct answer to fill the gaps (e.g. How do I decide which part of speech must fit into the gap?, How do I decide which type of past tense form of a verb or which singular or plural noun fits in the gap?). The FL educator cannot assume that a bright dyslexic FL student will work out these thinking steps on his or her own. The difficulty or sheer inability to do so is a characteristic phenomenon of dyslexia and must be recognised as such.

FL educators may be using test tasks not mentioned here. It is important to remember that this explicit focus on strategy instruction related to specific test tasks is absolutely necessary for dyslexic students to have even a fair chance of being successful. If not provided with such explicit test-taking strategy instruction, the dyslexic student will probably not be able to be successful in spite of having invested frequently more time than the good FL learner in preparing for the test. The frustrating result may then be – despite all efforts – another D or F grade. Especially in beginning level FL courses, the instructor may want to validate the effectiveness of the use of any of the presented strategies by pointing out that extra points will be given if these tools are being used appropriately during tests.

Monitoring test anxiety

Aside from concrete task-mastering strategies, managing test anxiety should be addressed openly as it belongs to a frequent painful reality of dyslexic (and non-dyslexic) FL learners. Among useful strategies are:

- modelling and providing practice in breathing techniques;

- modelling and allowing the use of a stress ball;

- a calming semi-vocalised mantra (e.g. 'I can do this!', ' I know this!', 'Fear go away. I do not need you');

- allowing the student, to approach the FL educator to tell him or her about the mental anxiety block in order to break the spell and then to be able to move on to the next task that seems manageable.

In addition to these suggestions, it may be useful to encourage the students themselves to contribute strategies that have helped them before. Explicitly addressing this issue in a relaxed, serious, respectful manner and allowing students to talk to the FL educator during the test may remove many anxiety factors at the start.

Careful selection of test tasks

FL skill testing typically involves written and oral tests. Each type contains a variety of tasks increasing in complexity the more advanced the course. First, written and then oral exam tasks are examined for use with dyslexic FL students. It should be noted that, to date, no detailed FL literature, that reflects thoroughly on the process, exists that addresses the special needs of an increasing number of students with more or less severe language processing difficulties in FL classes. The following suggestions are based on the first author's years of experience with this population in FL classes.

Written exam tasks

It is common for written FL tests to include any of the following tasks:

- matching activities of synonyms, opposites or sentence clauses;

- texts with gaps that the student is to fill and provide evidence of specific grammatical, syntactical, and/or semantic knowledge (cloze procedure);

- short sentence responses to small paragraph responses to picture scenes that engage the student in using certain newly learned vocabulary, grammatical and syntactical concepts;

- foreign culture questions.

The first suggestion with regard to dyslexic students' language processing difficulties is to **avoid cloze procedure tasks** whenever possible. Even in their native language, these students rely heavily on context clues (Pressley 2002). Asking these students to fill in the grammatically correct missing word or word part, even if choices are provided, places them in frustrating situations, preventing them from demonstrating what they really know. In the Ganschow, Philips and Schneider study (2000), dyslexic students repeatedly supported this view. They felt reduced to making wild guesses rather than being able to provide intelligent, knowledge-based answers. Second, for some dyslexic students with more severe visual processing difficulties, providing evidence of their actual knowledge in **matching activities** may be **difficult** and unfair, because their poor visual perceptual short-term memory is over-challenged by the specific eye-movement task required to match the combined word or sentence parts. Third, any FL text-writing task can be a stumbling block for dyslexic students. **Writing** is a multifaceted task that demands high concentration on content and frequently takes place for the dyslexic student at the cost of correct spelling, correct sentence structure and often also appropriate word choice in the FL. Since this **problem** occurs due to the nature of dyslexia and not due to sloppiness, the FL educator has to decide to what extent to count spelling, sentence structure/and or word choice errors in comparison to overall text structure and presented content.

Overall, in tests, students with dyslexia will profit from picture cues and opportunities to express their linguistic and cultural knowledge in alternative ways, including their native language if necessary. They will need extensive practice in written performance to feel comfortable with FL writing test tasks.

Oral exam tasks

It is common for oral FL tests to include any of the following tasks:

- listening to a tape section and responding through check marks or one's own words briefly in the FL to stated questions;

- listening to the FL educator speak in the FL and asking questions to which the student responds on paper with check marks or one's own words briefly in the FL;

- listening to the FL educator dictate words, phrases and/or sentences and responding on paper (classic dictation);

- an FL oral interview with an FL educator in which the student listens and responds in the FL to questions and non-verbal cues (sometimes pictures).

The first suggestion with regard to dyslexic students' oral language processing skills is to avoid an **immediate forced oral response**. Dyslexic students always need considerably more time to process a proposed or to be proposed question than their non-dyslexic peers. Dealing with a foreign instead of the native language intensifies this problem. Often it helps to supply the ongoing oral dialogue in class simultaneously with pictures and gestures as dyslexic learners process pictures better than letters and sounds.

Another option is to give students the questions **ahead of time** in written form so that they can prepare for a response and are not caught off guard. When two students are to prepare a dialogue together for an oral test grade, the FL educator should make an effort to consider personality and skill-level of the dyslexic student's team partner to guarantee success for both participants. Oral test parts that include listening to a tape or the FL instructor (e.g. dictations) followed by required written responses, and under time pressure, pose definite problems for dyslexic students and require modifications. They include, but are not limited to, proctoring these test parts separately in a **one-on-one situation** (assistant, tutor) which allows for repetition of oral information to accommodate the characteristically slower auditory processing skills of dyslexic students. **Visual clues** that go along with watching the speaker pronounce the words may provide another helpful accommodation in this setting. The written **response sheets** may be enlarged to make the visual processing of the print easier and/or they may be supported by additional pictures to provide more intense context clues. A drastic accommodation may consist of allowing the dyslexic student to provide an oral answer in the native language instead of responding on paper or orally in the FL. This last suggestion may be the only beneficial accommodation for more severely affected dyslexics.

In general, for oral or written test tasks alike, the FL educator can increase dyslexic students' chances to demonstrate what they know by providing the task instruction in the native instead of in the foreign language. While all students may profit from this accommodation, it is the dyslexic student who due to the specific auditory/visual processing difficulties may not be able to even attempt the completion of a given task without this translation accommodation. It might be most relevant to consider in beginning FL courses and could be provided either orally or written. In addition, the authors suggest that an FL tutor support and guide the dyslexic student's study and test taking efforts. For most beneficial results, the tutor should be familiar with the specific multisensory structured, metacognitive strategies that are most helpful for the student and are being reinforced by the FL teacher.

Appropriate test-taking modifications

Once students have learned test preparation and test-taking strategies, and proper test tasks have been chosen, the instructor needs to be aware of a variety of test accommodation strategies for the actual test-taking procedure. Strong and weak learning channels as well as details regarding strengths and weaknesses in processing linguistic information need to be considered carefully when selecting accommodations for the benefit of the student. Options should include the following five modifications.

Extended time

The most essential accommodation is to provide students with extended time to complete the test. It is important to note that only students who have studied their material properly will profit from extended time and be able to demonstrate their knowledge. This applies for dyslexic and non-dyslexic students alike. However, for dyslexic students who process language tasks by nature of their disability considerably slower than non-dyslexic learners, this accommodation will provide the otherwise missing opportunity to demonstrate their actual knowledge. Without extended time, dyslexic students always run out of time completing tasks. Additionally, trying to rush through tasks together with higher anxiety and frustration levels increase mistakes overall. Overall, extended time provides dyslexic students with a realistic chance to apply their test-taking and self-correction strategies and to demonstrate their actual knowledge much like their non-dyslexic peers.

A separate and/or distraction-free room

The next most useful accommodation provides dyslexic students with the opportunity to complete the test in a separate, quiet room with minimal auditory and visual distractions. If that is impossible in the given learning environment, then it will be beneficial to provide a test-taking 'niche' in a vision-blocked, separate section of the classroom (e.g. desk turned to a clear wall in the back of the classroom).

Alternative test modi

Another option to address the extended time and quiet environment aspect is to allow for the dyslexic student to complete a certain test part or the entire test as a **take-home exam**. The oral listening/writing response and the oral listening/oral response tasks can be completed independently by sending those parts home with the student on tape. This allows the student to listen to tasks and information as many times as needed until ready to record the proper answers on tape. It is important to note, however, that this audio tape alternative resembles the old-fashioned language laboratory situation. It has proven not to be the most beneficial learning and testing environment for dyslexic students with generally poor auditory processing skills, because listening and responding to and onto an audio tape activate only their poor auditory processing skills and thus would set these types of dyslexic FL learners up for failure from the start. For dyslexic students with normal auditory processing skills, the take-home audio tape alternative is a welcome option to be able to show FL knowledge and circumvent the problems likely in responding quickly to give oral responses.

The **computer** presents another option to accommodate dyslexic students' needs for extended time and a distraction-free environment to complete the exam. This option is especially beneficial for students with poor handwriting because they do not have to worry about letter formation and can concentrate on content. If the computer has the appropriate multimedia equipment, the student can also complete the oral listening/writing and oral listening/oral response part without requiring an invigilator next to him or her by listening to the recorded voice and responding to the oral questions. This oral test computer alternative may be considered with caution, however, since the voice recording qualities of programs differ greatly and if not really clear may cause more confusion than relief in a test situation.

Overall, the last two 'take home' versions are only a desirable option if the home environment is supportive, providing the quiet space needed to complete the test assignments.

A scribe or a reader

A scribe or a reader is a frequently used accommodation in native language test-taking situations for more severely affected dyslexic learners. It is known that dyslexic students with poor visual processing skills will be able to show what they really know about the subject area, when instructions to complete any test task are read aloud to them by a reader. Such accommodation is best provided in an environment where it does not disturb the other test-takers. Accommodations of this kind can vary in intensity from having the entire test invigilated individually with clarification of items in the native language in a separate room by a reliable invigilator, to having only task instructions quietly read to the student when requested by the student. A scribe would accommodate dyslexic students with severe visual processing difficulties and poor fine-motor skills that result in illegible handwriting. In addition, the memory problems of dyslexic students inevitably result also in spelling difficulties with sometimes indecipherable presentations of words. These students would waste so much time and energy on forming letters and attempting unknown or forgotten spelling rules that they would lose track of focusing on issues of content, completion of sentences and/or comprehension. A scribe takes away this pressure so that the student can concentrate on the actual content issues of the exam.

Colour-coded or white cards to plan sentence or text writing

An accommodation for sentence writing tasks in exams is to allow students to use their own laminated, clear and clean **colour-coded or white cards** to lay out the sentences before writing them down on the actual test sheet so that they can apply multi-sensory, metalinguistic processing tools to arrive at the best possible response.

When entire paragraphs are expected, the colour-coded text structure cards can be used as well (adapted from Auman 2002). Once designed and written out on coloured cards in full sentences, students can take a picture of their paragraph with a Polaroid instant picture **camera**. During the exam, this saves time and helps the students avoid producing errors when copying the entire paragraph word for word from the cards to the actual test sheets. The teacher then grades the written products based on the text captured on the photos. If this accommodation is not an option, students can tape their sentence strips together and hand in their text in a big envelope rather than on a regular sheet. It is the authors' opinion that this kind of explicitly constructive completion of a text writing task shows just as explicitly as non-colour and non-card writing the ability to produce cohesive, coherent text. Gradually, students with dyslexia are expected to be able to switch to paper and pencil if this transition phase during tests is allowed as an option.

In conclusion, teaching and practising a combination of test preparation, test-taking strategies, openly discussing advantages and disadvantages with the students involved as well as being open to experimenting with a variety of test-taking accommodations, will satisfy the FL educator and his or her students of all ability levels. It will allow for a more relaxed, open and exploratory learning environment in which all students have an equal chance of success.

Chapter 6

Technology and its Benefits for Dyslexic Students

How technology can enhance success in foreign language learning

The twenty-first-century virtual learning environment brings with it a whole new structure to foreign language learning and teaching. Through international exposure to the whole range of languages and cultures, the learner can experience at first hand the authentic atmosphere of 'living the language'. No longer does the classroom limit social communication to listening, speaking, reading and writing within the environs of the classroom with only the benefit of one or two foreign language educators' language performance as models. Rather, today's FL educators frequently use a variety of electronically based technological resources in bringing authentic FL experiences into their classrooms. FL students may spend several hours a week listening and responding to real voices in the foreign language of their choice. The most modern form of this FL experience represents the online multimedia FL experience of watching and responding to viewed information on video clips or video films in the foreign language. Accompanying writing assignments may be forwarded online to the FL instructor. Among other frequently used resources are audio tapes with authentic FL voices, use of copyrighted TV series presenting authentic foreign language features and the culture of the language being studied. German examples would be the detective series *Derrick* or family stories with a rich exposure to everyday cultural and linguistic information such as *Forsthaus Falkenau*. An example of a type of French humour is the detective series 'Inspector Clouseau', known in English as the 'Pink Panther' series. These visual and auditory examples provide FL learners with authentic FL and foreign culture information far beyond that which the FL educator could provide on his/her own. Further, it is common to use CD-ROM programs that accompany a given FL teaching series. These typically provide students with additional language practice related to specific grammatical, semantic and socio-pragmatic issues. On a regular basis FL educators may also assign web-based tasks to their students. These require students to access foreign language web sites to gain cultural information while practising reading comprehension skills in the foreign language. These tasks frequently also require students to transfer and apply this newly gained information in text compositions of varying degrees of complexity. Frequently, e-pal connections are established so that FL students practise authentic written communication skills in the FL. Often these lead to lifelong friendships and opportunities to visit each other. Access to authentic radio announcements and radio programmes has allowed FL educators to frequently include assignments into their curriculum that engage FL learners in analysing up-to-date political and cultural events.

While all these technology-based activities are becoming commonplace in today's FL classrooms, they have not been designed with the needs of students with language processing difficulties in mind. Given the fact that FL experiences are a component of primary/elementary and secondary education in most parts of the world (and to an increasing degree in the USA), we must now consider both the challenges and the benefits of our new tools for those with language processing difficulties such as dyslexia. Traditionally, FL education has not given particular consideration to these students as their regular participants. In today's FL classrooms of about 20–25 students, the FL educator can usually find between two and five students with differing degrees of language processing problems (Schneider 1999). Without specific and repeated guidance, these students can find themselves at a complete loss with many of these technology-supported tasks. Even then, some technology-based materials might be inappropriate for students with severe language processing difficulties unless the primary programme resources are carefully adapted for the capabilities of dyslexic FL students. It is essential therefore to examine the content and adaptability of frequently used electronic technological tools critically with regard to their adaptability towards specific needs of dyslexic FL learners. To date, the authors are unaware of such careful, critical analysis with the exception of a few anecdotal references from teachers who have taken it upon themselves to start writing interactive training materials for students with language processing difficulties on their own. To date, very little of this material has been published. The multimedia educational Rogers Center for Learning in California, USA, has been experimenting with multimedia FL and second language programs for Spanish, Japanese, Korean and other FLs. The Kurtzweil company has also been experimenting with multimedia programs for Spanish as a foreign language (personal conversation of the first author with representative, Canada, October 2000). These approaches are rare and need to be followed up with careful studies regarding their user-friendliness and effectiveness for dyslexic students in FL learning situations. To date, the authors know of no body of research that compares the effects of the technological media designed for students with dyslexia with those that were not specifically designed for this population. Certain parameters need to be considered. These must include: a) time spent with the technological tool as a tool that supports learning or as an initial teaching tool; b) amount of time spent with tool; c) type of linguistic processing difficulties (e.g. mainly visual or mainly auditory and/or attention deficit); d) the characteristics of the accompanying classroom FL instruction; and e) match/coincidence of classroom activities with the activities presented via the technological learning tools. A substantial body of research data would provide insight into what specifically needs to accompany good FL instruction for dyslexic students. Until we have that body of research evidence, we must rely on our own instincts and experiences to provide the tools 'to do the magic trick'. Exploration through a trial and error approach will have to guide our early progress in establishing best practice in the use of technology in our classrooms. The teacher needs to know what has been designed with the specific needs of dyslexic students in mind and what has just happened to suit certain individual dyslexic students. The following ideas provide the FL educator with information about the user-friendliness and adaptability of some frequently used technological resources. This chapter also provides suggestions about how to integrate technologies previously used in the field of special education only into the FL classroom to increase dyslexic students' success in the FL. These suggestions are based on both authors' experiences. Some of these are currently being piloted in the UK and the USA.

It is not only conceptual understanding that is needed for dyslexic students to gain mastery of a language. There are other principles of learning and teaching which need to be integrated into the programme to increase the probability of success. Some of the main features of technological resources that can make a positive difference in learning an FL for dyslexic students are the following:

- **independent access** to a resource at a time that is convenient for the student (e.g. independent computer access outside of the constraints of school hours);

- facility to pace the resource in such a way that there can be as **many repetitions** as are needed for the student to experience success and understanding;

- as much **overlearning** through a variety of technological and other resources as the student wishes;

- facility to **slow down the speed** at which spoken language is presented (especially important when it is an auditory resource only such as audio tape) and/or at which speed written language proceeds;

- integration of as **many learning channels** as possible, especially the kinaesthetic-tactile (move-touch) so that the dyslexic student can accommodate for possible weak auditory and/or visual processing skills. Support of the auditory channel with visual clues (e.g. video/book pictures) is the minimum needed for some success for the FL student with dyslexia. Note that the kinaesthetic-tactile component is frequently missing or not integrated strongly enough.

When judging the usefulness of electronically based FL learning material or other learning and teaching resources, the FL educator should examine the material for these features. If they are insufficient, any or a combination of the following accommodation ideas can be applied to increase the likelihood of success for the dyslexic FL learner (or any other student with similar language processing difficulties):

- **Add or strengthen the kinaesthetic-tactile learning component** to selected computer assignments (especially at the beginning level). Examples of such kinaesthetic-tactile learning enhancements might be asking the dyslexic student to trace over difficult words or word parts on the computer screen or on the mouse pad while pronouncing them slowly. Involving the strong kinaesthetic-tactile learning channel helps reinforce learning and helps the student memorise correct answers or difficult information (e.g. meaning and spelling or grammar). The FL educator may want to request tracing pads that are electronically connected to the screen, so that dyslexic students can see the letters they are tracing on the pad being traced on the screen as well.

- **Design activities** with repeated practice opportunities **that integrate multi-sensory practice**, especially integrating kinaesthetic-tactile components, with non-technological tools such as writing, tracing and saying, thinking aloud about problematic areas in vocabulary acquisition and/or grammar using pens, markers and/or coloured paper (see Chapter 3).

- **Ensure** that dyslexic FL students (or better still, *all* students) have **access to computer-based and CD-ROM-based exercise opportunities** outside of school hours restrictions to guarantee maximum practice time, especially for those students who do not have computer access at home. If the student finds it motivating, independent work can be stimulated by using programs that record the hours a student spends practising activities and/or using resources, and rewarding students for their investment and efforts. Even without a computer-based scoring system, FL educators are encouraged to develop a reward system for independent study time spent with technological resources to help the dyslexic student overcome the initial hurdles of negative experiences and feeling 'dumb' because they need to spend so much time in unrewarding study.

- Pair each dyslexic student with a well-performing FL learner who is capable and willing to help accommodate the dyslexic student during technology-based FL activities. Here, the teams can practise thinking aloud strategies as suggested in Chapter 3. This reinforces multi-sensory learning for both partners. Any strategy of suitable pairing of dyslexic students will result in more social and less lonely and frustrating experiences when using technological learning tools such as the computer or FL audio tapes.

- **Allow extended time** for dyslexic students to complete computer-based or web-based assignments to enable them to process the authentic language information given to them through repeated practice and opportunities to revise assignments.

Analysis of frequently used electronic technologies

Taking advantage of electronic tools that are commonly used in FL classrooms and electronic devices that were originally designed for native language instruction helps ensure that students receive the maximum opportunity to engage in motivating technology-based self-study practices. This teaches them confidence and independence in acquiring FL skills and the most up-to-date knowledge about foreign culture. Further, electronic technologies allow dyslexic students to work at an individual pace without being ridiculed by better performing peers.

CD-ROMs

Computer software in the form of CD-ROMs enables pupils to work at their own level and pace using media that encourage personal engagement with the language material without the necessity for the FL educator's presence. Independent learning can be stimulated while at the same time providing essential opportunities for repetition to reach automaticity in a specific language task. Natural voice speech models native speaker pronunciation. This learning tool provides the shy or uncertain FL learner with the protection of being able to repeat and practise FL expressions and pronunciation features without necessarily being overheard by other students. Further, the dyslexic learner may prefer FL practices via use of CD-ROMs because the CD-ROM materials may present themselves as the 'more patient FL teacher' that never needs to chastise pupils for making an error but rather responds positively and encourages corrections. Such 'error-friendly' learning environments without (often disabling) peer-pressure motivate struggling students to continue to practise and improve their skills. At present, there are a considerable number of CD-ROMs available for various foreign languages that attempt to support such motivating, independent FL study and practice at different skill levels. The FL educator should keep in mind, however, that at present CD-ROM materials for foreign language learning have not been written and marketed specifically for dyslexic students in the FL classroom. Therefore, additional accommodations for success in an FL may be required, especially for students with more severe and more complex language processing difficulties.

While individual CD-ROMs will provide attractive, multi-sensory learning material and can be structured around individual lessons, complete FL teaching courses can be downloaded from the Internet for various languages. For dyslexic FL students such entire Internet versions of FL programs are all the more effective if they fulfil a variety of criteria. It is helpful if:

1. The program contains **visual clues** that are closely linked to the language information given.

2. The program offers **kinaesthetic-tactile learning activities** and concrete, explicitly modelled **mnemonic study devices** for pronunciation, grammar and vocabulary acquisition.

3. The program progresses in **small steps**, providing frequent opportunities for revision and much thinking-aloud and multi-sensory learning. Explicit initial instruction on how to complete specific CD-ROM tasks is also needed as well as continuous availability for guidance and facilitation through thought-provoking questions (see Chapter 3) until the dyslexic student has reached a level of proficiency and confidence with the FL material.

The FL educator is also advised to contact the British, European or International Dyslexia Association for new editions of dyslexic-needs-based FL CD-ROM material. In the USA, several programs are currently being piloted for accuracy and user-friendliness for dyslexic students. See the section Resources.

Digital language instruction

While there are many individual CD-ROMs available that FL

students can use independently at home or on class computers, there are classroom systems that do not require the FL student to use a computer at all. So-called **digital language instruction** refers to a technological learning tool that allows FL students to work with their FL educator using specifically designed audio panels. The teacher uses a computer and controls the activities that the students are doing. Teachers can plan different activities and different methods for each session. The teacher can work with one student or an entire class and lessons can be planned so that each student is working at his or her own level to receive maximum personal benefit from the assigned activities. When the FL teacher's microphone is 'live', the computer displays it as being 'On the air'. The student then can hear the teacher's voice through the computer. This technological tool allows the teacher to assess individually in which phase of the programme each student is working at a given time. Pre-programmed activities direct both the teacher and the student through work at their own specific level. Activities can include any of the following in any sequence:

- **Listening comprehension**: Students work at their own pace operating their digital recorders individually listening to digital text as many times as needed to then be able to answer questions posed either by the FL educator or by other FL learners in the class.

- **Reading practice**: Students read aloud and then listen to their computer recordings. They learn to evaluate their own oral reading performance and try to improve their pronunciation, fluency or any other feature during the next practice round.

- **Model imitation**: The FL educator sets the model for teaching students proper stress, rhythm and intonation of the FL. The students repeat and practise using these models, play back the recordings of their own responses and learn to evaluate their own performance to improve at the next try.

- **Phone conversations**: Students call one another and practise conversing on the phone using their audio record panels.

- **Paired and group discussions**: Students role-play and express their views about a given topic in the FL. They also learn to act appropriately in simulated settings of intercultural communication.

- **Simultaneous and consecutive interpreting**: Students interpret text content either consecutively or simultaneously as the teacher reads. Student interpretations are recorded on the computer for later evaluation.

- **Recorded responses**: Students act as appropriately as possible in response to a pre-recorded source. Situations/dialogues such as job interviews, doctor's visits or room bookings can be presented. Individual responses can later be evaluated and scored by the computer or by the FL educator personally.

- **Tests**: The teacher assesses at a glance a student's performance level by viewing computer graphs of the test results.

A variety of CD-ROMs has been used in the past to assist dyslexic students' improvements in reading, writing and spelling skills in their native language English. Since these all contain a strong multi-sensory component and are carefully structured in small learning units, they provide multiple opportunities for review. These resources are a valuable additional learning tool which is specifically suited to dyslexic learners of English as an FL. Even though these programs have not been specifically designed for foreign or second language instruction, their scope and sequence in topics and activities sometimes provide a missing link of practice opportunities for the dyslexic student. Particularly useful are the specific multi-sensory letter-sound awareness training components for which the regular FL curriculum traditionally does not take much time: programs such as 'Climbing with Phonics', a multi-sensory CD-ROM program containing interactive multimedia video, text, authentic human voices and music to engage students at varying levels in sound/letter-based and syllable-based auditory and visual training activities in preparation for following spelling dictation activities, handwriting videos, phonic cloze stories, vocabulary development activities, sentence and paragraph writing skills and dictionary skills. It is important to note that overall all FL students can profit from these special interactive, truly multi-sensory learning activities but the dyslexic English as a foreign or second language student will profit most from them. These programs are available for school use and private use. (See the section on Resources.)

While some FL educators and FL learners might argue that this 'digital experience' is artificial, many FL students feel self-conscious about their oral performance. Often these less successful FL students prefer the individual practice opportunity in a private and secure situation, free of degrading and humiliating experiences in comparison with well-performing peers. Further, the FL educator has the flexibility to allow every FL student to progress as fast as each student's language processing skills allow them, so keeping individual differences confidential.

Internet and web sites

For FL educators, the Internet provides a variety of authentic FL teaching resources. Freely downloadable clip art provides teachers with opportunities to support often abstract grammatical information with concrete pictures that serve as mnemonic devices to aid the comprehension of difficult linguistic information. (See Tables 3.4a and 3.4b on pictures and drawings and Table 3.9 on personifications in Chapter 3.) It is important for FL educators to monitor and screen any sites carefully before encouraging students to use them as, apart from avoiding unprofessional information, the content may also be age-inappropriate. The web site information must be simple and clearly structured. Busy, small print and overcrowded web sites cause overstimulation and confusion for FL students with dyslexia. Pictures are most supportive in the FL language learning progress, when clearly linked with the text provided next to them. When selecting Internet sites for FL assignments, it is helpful to also have a variety of foreign culture web sites available for the dyslexic student that are written in the student's native language. This provides a back-up resource for students who are struggling and for situations in which the FL sites are too overwhelming for dyslexic students to cope with the information in the timely fashion required for a given assignment. The FL educator may want to join the Centre for Information on Language Teaching and Research (CILT) web site (see the section on Resources). This organisation runs a discussion forum to generate ideas and mutual support for all those who are involved in teaching modern foreign languages to students with additional support needs in mainstream classes.

For the FL student with dyslexia, integrating the use of the Internet and web sites into FL assignments offers several advantages, provided the foreign language sites are chosen carefully and/or the dyslexic FL learner has been advised how to deal with a confusing web site. Some helpful strategies to refer to when encountering a website with overwhelming information may be:

- skimming for important information with a peer using pre-established key-questions;

- making the FL educator aware of difficulties with web site and ask for assistance or permission to search for a native language web site with similar information to be able to gain the content information relevant for the assignment in a timely fashion;

- searching for different foreign language web sites.

Most of all, the Internet provides the dyslexic student with access to cultural information in native and/or the foreign language so that the student with language processing difficulties can acquire a wealth of FL cultural knowledge and bicultural awareness necessary to become a better informed global citizen. If the FL educator allows students with dyslexia to share their newly gained cultural knowledge in the native language rather than the foreign language, the otherwise disadvantaged student can compensate for poor linguistic processing skills with high-quality performance regarding foreign cultural knowledge and critical, reflective thinking regarding differences and similarities between two cultures. Further, the fact that web sites are frequently supported by pictures, often moving pictures supported by sound effects, provides a multi-sensory FL learning tool with authentic language exposure which provides the dyslexic student with opportunities to compensate for specific language processing weaknesses.

The Internet: electronic bulletin boards and email

Electronic **bulletin boards**, sometimes referred to as 'blackboards', present a useful FL study and teaching tool for students and teachers alike. A frequent accommodation for dyslexic students in native language classes is the sharing of notes with peers and/or the classroom teachers. In some cases, teacher and student have worked out an arrangement that allows the student access to the lesson overheads and teacher's notes prior to the actual class in which the topic is being covered. This way, the student can prepare for the topic ahead of time, compensating for slow language processing skills and maximising effective learning time in class. The electronic bulletin board provides an opportunity for FL educators to provide such information prior to class or at least after class for students with dyslexia. Further, the FL educator can post reading assignments of various levels of challenge for different skill levels of students to provide differentiated instruction and homework practice. Students can learn to use bulletin boards to post contributions which they have prepared (perhaps with help) beforehand. **Emails** and **web pages** can be used to promote writing and reading skills in the FL. Email can also be used effectively for individually written test assignments in or outside of class (see Chapter 5). The opportunity to type responses to test questions rather than writing them by hand provides an enormous relief and reduction of spelling and grammar errors for students with dyslexia who may display poor handwriting skills. Further, the FL **spellchecker** can be used and revisions are easier to make because erasing is unproblematic on the electronic screen. FL educators who fear preferential treatment of dyslexic students in the FL classroom can relax. Despite this accommodation, the dyslexic students' language processing difficulties will still cause errors. One should remember that a spellchecker can only be used successfully if the original spelling is close enough to the correct one and, in case of the FL, the student can choose the correct vocabulary word from a list of similar-looking words. These are all challenges for students with dyslexia. With this accommodation, however, they have a better chance of demonstrating to what extent they have understood foreign language components at least conceptually. **E-pal exchanges** encourage pupils with dyslexia to participate in authentic intercultural exchange using the FL skills available to them. The first author suggests experimenting with European e-pals who also suffer from language processing difficulties but are learning English as a foreign language. This puts all participants in comparable situations and gives them topics to share. Anecdotal tales of a small pilot project of this kind between 12 German students of English and 12 American dyslexic students reported positive, highly motivating and even continuing e-pal connections.

Videos or DVDs

Because videos can provide FL learners with the facility to review material as often as they wish, they can be used as a reinforcement to class work for replay at home. Videos/DVDs are of help to dyslexic students, because they present the language supported with a series of visual clues (pictures). Videos/DVDs in which actions and language are closely linked work best for FL learners, and dyslexic learners in particular, because action reinforces/translates language and vice versa. When films, news, or reports show subtitles in the foreign language, the dyslexic student receives a multisensory written and oral, as well as non-verbal, foreign-language and culture input. While the dyslexic FL learner may need to preview and/or post-view film material shown in class many times and also with slowed down pace, the non-dyslexic learners can just enjoy viewing video tapes/DVDs at regular pace. Foreign language laboratories provide easy access to multiple viewing opportunities and a variety of accommodations (time, pace, space). Thus, videos/DVDs are an effective multisensory tool to support the FL educator in differentiating FL instruction according to individual differences. Providing dyslexic FL learners with guiding questions when viewing videos/DVDs in an FL, will be highly beneficial for increasing their comprehension skills. It has proved to help dyslexic FL students initially to get pointed towards identifying and using language and picture-related information properly through explicit questions such as: What does ... *do* after the teacher frowned at her and said something? What do you think the teacher said, based on Tina's reaction?

Initially, it also helps to explicitly encourage the dyslexic FL learner to use the slow-down features available. These suggestions are not conclusive but provide the reader with a spectrum of ideas.

While the previously identified technological resources have traditionally been used in FL classrooms, the following suggestions include those that originally have been used successfully in native language instruction with dyslexic students but have been found beneficial for dyslexic students in FL learning situations. Some technological tools have newly added FL features and thus offer helpful study materials for dyslexic students in FL classrooms. It is essential to note that it is the FL educator's responsibility to introduce the struggling FL learner to these tools explicitly to maximise learning success.

Dyslexia-sensitive computer software

Computer software from 'Kurzweil' originally designed as learning tools for students with visual and reading disabilities has now been made available for FL learners. 'Kurzweil 3000', for instance, can read FL texts in a number of European languages, and help design text structure outlines translate between these languages and English. This provides a superb learning tool for dyslexic FL learners, especially those who struggle with decoding/reading text. Different language versions of programs such as 'ViaVoice' or 'Dragon Naturally Speaking' allow students to hear the language being read aloud to them by native speakers of the FL. Dictation into the computer may be problematic as some dyslexic students' pronunciation may be too poor for the computer to recognise the appropriate words and to display the correct ones. Further, **Optical Character Recognition** (OCR) can allow students to scan in a specific language and to have it read back accurately, helping with the improvement of FL pronunciation issues and giving pupils access to more challenging sentence and word patterns than they would otherwise be able to handle with confidence. It is, however, for the student to decide if the benefits from such software are worth the effort. They must allow sufficient time to fully try out and see the potential of such programs. Additionally, computer programs can further facilitate learning by: a) helping with graphic organisation and planning of language concepts, FL test and homework tasks, grouping vocabulary into semantically related word families or according to prefix or suffix patterns, or b) organising grammatical information into attractive layouts to enhance strong picture reading skills are an essential learning tool for dyslexic students in FL classes. The program 'Inspiration' offers such teaching and learning tools. This program also offers useful tools for the FL educator to provide visually attractive graphic organisers for lesson plans so that the dyslexic student can understand language concepts more easily via the picture-type graphic organisers.

Dyslexia-sensitive dictionaries, translators and spellcheckers

The Franklin Company has supported dyslexic students with successful learning tools for many years by offering electronic **dictionaries**, **translators** and **spelling correctors** in little hand-held calculator-type machines which provide the proper spelling for a word keyed into the machine, or alternative vocabulary like a thesaurus, and also translate into the language specified. When the dyslexic student is able to provide accurate enough pronunciation and/or spelling of the word, these can be a saving grace for students with learning difficulties. The company offers these language tools also for FL learning, including bilingual translation features so that students can quickly access a translation and/or spelling of a word in an FL. They can also provide a guide to grammar and give common phrases that are likely to be used in the other language.

Other translation tools such as the speaking 'Quicktionary pen' have been used to help students with learning difficulties in their native language for many years. When unfamiliar with the pronunciation of a word, the student scans over the word with the pen. The pen then provides the pronunciation. This feature is now also available for some foreign languages. In addition to providing the pronunciation, the pen will also translate the meaning of the word into the native language. This is a time-efficient tool for dyslexic students who usually are extremely slow and often inaccurate in using dictionaries due to their slow language processing skills. Spelling difficulties and problems over sequencing or copying can be ignored as well, as the dyslexic person gains all the benefits of a paper dictionary without the stress attached to finding a word in the 'real' dictionary.

Tape recorders and books on tape

There are still many benefits to be gained from the use of the humble tape recorder. While this may no longer be considered to be at the forefront of modern technology, nonetheless the benefits of the tape for the dyslexic student are still recognisable. The tape can function as **note-taker** for dyslexic students with good auditory processing skills. Recording class instructions allows the dyslexic student to listen to the content of the lesson repeatedly. Thus it can support vocabulary learning, substitute for often slow and erroneous note-taking, and function as an individual response tool between the dyslexic student and the FL educator as the student can record oral responses after repeated practice and submit the tape to the FL educator when the task is completed. This way the FL educator can receive some oral language data on dyslexic students without forcing them to respond spontaneously in class and setting them up for failure. Homework assignments can also be completed by the student offering oral answers instead of written responses, if this is an appropriate accommodation for a particular dyslexic student. Opportunities for overlearning through repeated playbacks while seeing the word(s) presented visually in print will give maximum benefit for the dyslexic student with visual processing difficulties, making the experience a multi-sensory one.

A special use of tape recorders may involve the use of 'books-on-tape' accommodations. These accommodations have scarcely been provided for dyslexic students in FL classrooms. The first author has personally followed the learning success of one dyslexic student in an introductory college Spanish class. The student had requested the entire Spanish language learning book on tape, the audio-tape materials included. Knowing his auditory strengths and relying on his previous success with books-on-tape in English language classes in high school, he designed his own study programme based on the tape material and passed his Spanish 101 with a very good grade. An in-depth interview with the student revealed that he based his success mainly on knowing how to use the FL book in its 'book-on-tape version' (Schneider & Philips, 1999). Since 'books-on-tape,' or on CD are successful accommodations in native language instruction, especially at the secondary level in content areas such as biology, chemistry, social studies or history, its use in the FL learning environment is strongly encouraged. It provides the dyslexic student with multiple opportunities for independent study and self-correction.

Perimeter Audio Learning Equipment (PALE)

Perimeter Audio Learning Equipment (PALE) is a simple audio tape-based system which can be used around the classroom walls to reinforce language concepts at an individual or group level (e.g. grammar, pronunciation, spelling, vocabulary, conversations). Students work with headphones and are equipped with microphones. The system allows pupils to work in a normal classroom situation and to participate in listening and speaking activities at their own level. All of this work can be monitored and assisted by the class teacher. Such equipment is often underused. The opportunity to tailor learning pace and content to individual student needs or those of small groups is highly beneficial for the dyslexic FL learner. Also, the option to repeat practice sessions based on individual need is highly beneficial to the dyslexic student. Oral and auditory tasks can be conducted between students in the security of a small group environment where those who might otherwise be inhibited are not intimidated by the thought that they are being heard by a large group of people. It is also good to know that newer PALE systems are specially designed to withstand the rough treatment that pupils often give the machines. Although quite unsophisticated in the present day, overall the PALE system offers an effective non-threatening individualised addition to the FL educator's direct intervention.

The use of the Language Master

The Language Master is a teaching and learning tool commonly used in accommodating dyslexic students in acquiring native language reading skills. It consists of a tape recorder with headphones and an audio tape that accompanies a reading text to be followed simultaneously while listening to the text on tape. This is a more refined method of using tape recording in language education than the old-fashioned tape recorder or the PALE system. The teacher can listen to the student's performance at his or her convenience and analyse errors to plan needs-based instruction and the student has the opportunity to practise and go over the reading material with the tape repeatedly. This tool can be used successfully in FL learning situations. In addition to using the Language Master as described for accommodations in the native language, the FL student can listen to the teacher's voice (or other native speaker's voice) recorded on tape and practise improving pronunciation skills and reading skills (with text provided along with auditory information) and record his or her voice until satisfied with the result. Especially in the initial stages of practising with this learning tool, the FL educator should provide the dyslexic student with concrete suggestions as to where and how to improve specific areas of weakness. If there is an error, it is important to note here that dyslexic students must be shown explicitly how and why (the metacognitive component) the error must be corrected to avoid future errors. When dyslexic students use this tool to improve their FL pronunciation and reading skills, it is beneficial to keep a notebook of the specific areas of difficulty and correction devices suggested including metacognitive reasons for the correction. Thus, students can use their personal notes for self-correction reference. The first author has used this device with her FL students in introductory German as a foreign language classes and received positive feedback from her students regarding the usefulness of this record-keeping device along with the Language Master practice.

Conclusion

Despite the identified benefits of technology to enhance success in FL learning for dyslexic students, it is essential to keep the irreplaceable benefits of the active personal contact with the FL educator in and outside of the classroom in mind. The findings of the Ganschow, Philips and Schneider study (2000) support the importance of the personal contact with the FL educator especially for the dyslexic student. Every interviewed dyslexic student emphasised his or her dependence on the FL educator's personal guidance through the learning process. Further, FL educators will be challenged with the task to select from a great variety of technological FL resources that are not specifically designed to aid the dyslexic student in the FL learning process. These days, technological assistance for dyslexic learners in foreign/second language courses is still a pioneer field and requires close collaboration and discussion in and across countries between devoted FL educators and specialists across disciplines (e.g. learning disability specialists, linguists, speech pathologists, psychologists) as well as dyslexic students and their parents. The authors, therefore, advise FL educators to check with colleagues at their schools for availability of some of the technological tools originally used to work with dyslexic students on improving their native language skills. This chapter provides an introduction to this dialogue and hopes to initiate fruitful experiences for both FL educators and their students with language processing difficulties.

A list of resources is contained at the end of the book. It is not exhaustive but gives some ideas and samples of what is currently available.

Chapter 7

Conclusion

This book has introduced FL educators to a common, outwardly 'invisible' learning disability called 'dyslexia'. It has shared learning and teaching strategies for students showing symptoms of this disability. Some may already be classified officially, some may not. In addition, accommodation strategies promise to make inclusion of dyslexic students in the FL classroom a better and more fruitful experience. The book focuses on achievements in FL learning for students of all ages with dyslexia. It highlights probabilities of success, and identifies ways to increase the realistic chance of individuals with dyslexia gaining reasonable skills in common FL learning settings. Through a wide variety of strategies and techniques, it is often possible for the most severely affected students to gain some success and a feeling of achievement. The difficulties, however, should not be underestimated, and these likely problems have also been outlined with a view to increasing the FL educators' understanding of dyslexia. For many dyslexic students the learning of a foreign language causes considerable anxiety. However, for those who receive sympathetic teaching and appropriate strategies and accommodations, the rewards can be great in terms of personal satisfaction and increased communication. The rewards for the teachers also are not insignificant. To watch a student gain accomplishment in a foreign language though struggling with the amount of overlearning which is sometimes necessary can be a painful experience, but one that gives the teacher satisfaction in being a part of the long anticipated success.

The Introduction to the book provided the reader with an overview of the issues involved and an understanding of how dyslexia manifests itself. Chapter 1 introduced the reader to classic profiles of dyslexic students and case studies illustrating success. While the barriers to learning can lie both within the student and in the classroom environment, if one of these can be changed for the better, then it certainly should be. Chapter 2 focused on the particular barriers to foreign language learning for dyslexic students. For many FL educators, the desire to do the best for the student drives them to seek out as many ways as possible to increase the success of their students. Through teaching metacognitive strategies to students, and through teaching in a metacognitive way, students can find out how they learn best and then use that knowledge in learning in subjects across the curriculum. Chapter 3 introduced this concept of metacognition and ideas to integrate this essential aspect into FL instruction to lead dyslexic students to successful FL experiences. Chapter 4 shared strategies to increase dyslexic students' personal feeling of success in FL classes by engaging them in a variety of multi-sensory, structured, metalinguistic learning activities. These give promises of success, increase personal enjoyment in FL learning and thus 'make FL learning fun'. Chapter 5 presented a variety of ideas on how to improve dyslexic students' test scores. They included suggestions for explicit instruction in test preparation and test-taking skills, selection of least troublesome test tasks, and beneficial test-taking accommodations.

Technology too can be a valuable aid to students' learning and can act as teacher's helper at times when reinforcement is required or when patience is running low. The computer can take over and will never run out of patience. Whether used as a tool for the student or a tool for the teacher, the computer is a wonderful facilitator of learning. Through attractive programs, motivation increases and teachers can capitalise on the benefits of twenty-first-century technology which is increasing communication skills throughout the world. Chapter 6 provided suggestions for how to best use technology to accommodate dyslexic students' needs in the FL classroom.

From the information assimilated in the course of the book, the following implications can be drawn for a more successful FL teaching and learning experience for dyslexic students and their educators:

1. The FL educator must be willing to engage in 'different', multi-sensory, structured, metacognitive teaching, learning and/or

study strategies, even if they go against previously learned FL teaching strategies or pedagogical belief systems. The success of the student with dyslexia depends on each individual teacher's flexibility and willingness to expand his or her teaching and testing repertoire with appropriate strategies.

2. The FL educator must be willing to collaborate with all who are involved with the student: for example, the Learning Disability Coordinator, the school's educational psychologist, the parents and most of all the student himself or herself. If teacher and student engage in frequent, honest dialogue about learning progress and effectiveness of certain strategies, success in the FL will become a reality.

3. The suggested explicit teaching, testing, and study strategies and accommodations are neither common components of FL teacher training programmes nor of FL teacher development workshops. Therefore, future FL teacher and teacher aide training as well as continuing education workshops should be encouraged to apply the presented content to expand their pedagogical repertoire with teaching and testing strategies that recognise the reality of students with language processing difficulties in FL classes.

4. Success becomes a real opportunity for students with dyslexia when the suggested strategies and background information on dyslexia are fully considered. However, FL educators must be cautioned that sometimes a student may be so severely affected by language processing difficulties that despite all collaboration and accommodation of the type suggested in this book, the student will not succeed and will be unable to fulfil the FL requirements. This is a sad but true reality. For these students the only way to move forward may be to abandon the teaching of the FL for the time being. For some the struggle to achieve success may not prove to be a valuable use of time, and concentrating for some time on a subject other than a foreign language may be the best alternative. In some areas it may be possible to focus on classes and/or projects that introduce foreign cultural information in the native language through foreign literature in translation, history courses that introduce different cultures and countries, or social studies classes that

compare different cultures in various aspects. Such opportunities, for instance, exist for college students in various different countries (foreign language substitution courses). In lower grades, teachers should encourage these students to engage in foreign culture projects to still receive knowledge in and about cultural diversity.

In the twenty-first century with its trend towards global civilisation, every global citizen, dyslexics included, needs to possess cultural awareness. This includes knowledge about and respect for cultural differences. As members of a group of 'different people' themselves, dyslexic students might even be more inclined to attune to cultural diversity and associated additional support needs than successful FL learners who are not faced with mind-boggling linguistic hurdles.

The authors hope that this book has raised awareness among FL educators of the real existence of dyslexic students in FL classes. We hope it will encourage many FL educators across the world to experiment with new teaching and testing strategies that benefit struggling FL learners, and dyslexic students in particular. Finally, we hope that this book will have stimulated a dialogue about the need to meet a truly increasingly diverse student body in today's FL classes with the overall goal of independence in mind.

Resources

The following list is not exhaustive but gives some ideas and samples of what is currently available.

Contact organisations

British Dyslexia Association (BDA)
www.bda-dyslexia.org.uk

Centre for Information on Language Teaching and Research (CILT)
www.cilt.org.uk

Dyslexia Institute, UK
www.dyslexia-inst.org.uk/index.htm

European Dyslexia Association (EDA)
www.bedford.ac.uk/eda

International Dyslexia Association (IDA)
8600 LaSalle Rd
Chester Bldg./Suite 382
Baltimore MD 21286-2044
Tel: 410-296-0232
www.interdys.org
This source is good for updates on foreign language/second language teaching materials

Learning Disabilities Association (LDA) www.ldanatl.org

Scottish Centre for Information on Language Teaching and Research (SCILT)
www.scilt.stir.ac.uk

CD-ROM Resources

Interactive CD-ROMs/DVD-ROMs/on-line are available from:

Cybermind
www.cybermind.com

Edith Rose Products Ltd
St Stephen's Hall
Oxford Road
Windsor SL4 5DX

Education City
www.EducationCity.net

Eurotalk interactive
315–317 New King's Road
London SW6 4RF
www.eurotalk.co.uk

Inspiration
www.iansyst.co.uk or www.inspiration.com

Learning Company
www.learningcompany.com

Random House Publishers
www.randomhouse.com

Revilo
PO Box 71
Winchester SO21 1ZE
www.revilo.com
(French and German)

Softease
www.softease.com

Speaking Our Language
Cànan Limited
Sabhal Mòr Ostaig
Teangue Sleat
Isle of Skye IV44 8XA
www.canan.co.uk
(Scottish Gaelic)

FL program with multitude of electronic resources

- montgomery.cas.muohio.edu/ILRC/
  (Spanish, Latin, French, Italian, German)
- Project ALLADIN: enhances integration of computer-based
  resources in FL teaching; includes, e-pal connection FL tutor
  links, www.alladin.ac.uk for languages: EFL/ESL, French,
  German, Spanish, Portuguese.

Multisensory structured programmes and CD-ROMs for English as a foreign language

'Climbing with Phonics'
AB-CD ROM USA Inc.
9856 Lemonwood Drive
Boynton Beach
FL 33437
Tel: 1-800 9- PHONIC
Fax: 561-732-4692
www.ab-sdrom.com
This source offers an extra writing program on a separate floppy disk
as well as an instructional manual with word frequency lists from the
articles included on the CD-ROM.

Fingertip Books
6040 Ranlyn Ave
Cincinnati OH 45239
Tel: 513-923-3759
www.fingertipbooks.net
This source offers letter-sound awareness training materials and
spelling rules for English as a second/foreign language with a
teacher manual and student lesson/worksheets

Kurzweil Educational Systems
14 Crosby Drive
Bedford MA 01730-1402
Tel. from USA: 800-894-5374
Tel. from other countries: 781-276-0600
www.kurzweiledu.com
Fax: 781-276-0650

'Language Tune-Up Kit'
Order Department
JWor Enterprises Inc.
4254 Maryland Drive
Columbus OH 43224
Fax: 888-329-0407
www.jwor.com
(Spanish version, 2003)

The Rogers Center for Learning
388 Market Street
Suite 500
San Francisco
CA 94111
www.rogerscenter.com
e-mail: info@rogerscenter.com
This publisher is also experimenting with CD-ROMs in other
foreign languages such as Spanish

Senlac Language Publications
PO Box 94
St Leonards-on-Sea
East Sussex TN37 7ZW
www.senlac.com
This source offers crosswords, word searches and games on
CD-ROMs

Other resources

Books on tape

Each country has a centre for Recordings for the Blind. There,
professionals read any books on tape; check resources available in
your country.

Electronic dictionaries, translators and spelling correctors

A range of electronic dictionaries, translators and spelling correctors
for European languages is available from:

Franklin Electronic Publishers (UK) Ltd
11 and 12 Windmill Business Village
Brooklands Close
Sunbury-on-Thames
Middlesex TW16 7DY
www.franklin-uk.co.uk or www.franklin.com

Games

Miniflashcard Language Games (MLG) and activities from:

MLG Publishing
PO Box 1526
Hanwell London W7 1ND
Tel: 020 7567 1076

Language Master
Drake Educational Associates
St Fagans Road
Fairwater
Cardiff CF5 3AE
www.language-master.co.uk
Also: Scottish Learning Products
Highfield Road
Scone
Perth PH2 6BR

Audio-learning Equipment

Enhanced Language Instruction Centre (elice), a sophisticated PALE
system with only one computer required is available from:

Tandberg Educational
Divace Learning Solutions Ltd
PO Box 41
FIN-20741
Turku
Finland
www.divace.com

Perimeter Audio Learning Equipment (PALE) communicative language teaching for classroom situations is available from:

Keith Audio Ltd
Unit 9
Turner Dumbrell Workshops
North End
Ditchling
East Sussex BN6 8TD

Quicktionary Pen
www.dyslexic.com

Videos and Multimedia Foreign Language Courses

Videos
4Learning
PO Box 400
Wetherby LS23 7LG
(French, German and Spanish)

Longman Publishers
www.longman.com
(French, German, Spanish, Italian, English as a Foreign/Second Language)

Video and multimedia courses
Young Europeans Bookstore
5 Cecil Court
London WC2N 4EZ
(French, German, Portuguese, Italian, Russian and Spanish)

References

Augur, J. (1993) *Early Help: A Better Future.* Reading: British Dyslexia Association.

Auman, M. (2002) *Step Up to Writing* (2nd edn). Longmont, CO: Sopris West.

Bakker, D. J. (1990) *Neuropsychological Treatment of Dyslexia.* New York: Oxford University Press.

Birsh, J. (ed.) (1999) *Multisensory Teaching of Basic Language Skills.* Baltimore, MD: Paul Brookes Publishing.

Borokowski, J. G. (1992) 'Metacognitive theory: a framework for teaching literacy, writing and math skills'. *Journal of Learning Disabilities,* **25**, 253–7.

Bos, C. S., Anders, P. L., Filip, D. and Jaffe, L. E. (1989) 'The effects of an interactive instructional strategy for enhancing reading comprehension and content area learning for students with learning disabilities'. *Journal of Learning Disabilities,* **22**, 348–90.

British Psychological Society (BPS) (1999) *Dyslexia, Literacy and Psychological Assessment.* Report by Working Party of the Division of Educational and Child Psychology. Leicester: British Psychological Society.

Brown, A. (2000) *The How to Study Book.* New York: Barricade Books Inc.

Carroll, J. B., and Sapon, S. M. (1959) *Modern Language Aptitude Test (MLAT).* New York: Psychological Corporation.

Crombie, M. A. (1995) 'The effects of specific learning difficulties (dyslexia) on the learning of a foreign language in school'.

Dyslexia: An International Journal of Research and Practice, **3**(1), 27–47.

Crombie, M. (2002) 'Dyslexia: The New Dawn'. Unpublished doctoral thesis, Glasgow, Strathclyde University.

Crombie, M. and McColl, H. (2001) 'Dyslexia and the teaching of modern foreign languages', in Peer, L. and Reid, G. (eds), *Dyslexia and Inclusion in the Secondary School.* London: David Fulton Publishers, pp. 54–63.

Deshler, D. D., Shumaker, J. B. and Lenz, K. (1984a) 'Academic and cognitive interventions for learning disabled adolescents', Part I. *Journal of Learning Disabilities,* **17**, 108–17.

Deshler, D. D., Shumaker, J. B., Lenz, K. and Ellis, E. (1984b) 'Academic and cognitive interventions for learning disabled adolescents', Part II. *Journal of Learning Disabilities,* **17**, 170–9.

Doyle, J. (1996) *Dyslexia: An Introductory Guide.* London: Whurr Publishers.

Eames, F. H. (2002) 'Changing definitions and concepts of literacy: implications for pedagogy and research', in Reid, G. and Wearmouth, J. (eds), *Dyslexia and Literacy Theory and Practice.* Chichester, John Wiley, pp. 327–41.

Eccles, G. F. and Wigfield, A. (1985) 'Teacher expectation and student motivation', in Dusek, J. B. (ed.) *Teacher Expectancies.* Hillsdale, NJ: Erlbaum.

Ehrlich, I. (1968) *Instant Vocabulary: A Simple and Exciting Method that will Enable You to Understand Thousands of New Words Instantly – Even if You Have Never Seen Them Before.* New York: Pocket Books.

Ellis, D. (2000) *Becoming a Master Student* (8th edn). Boston, MA: Houghton Mifflin.

Ganschow, L., Philips, L. and Schneider, E. (2000) 'Experiences with the university foreign language requirement: voices of students with learning disabilities', *Learning Disabilities: A Multidisciplinary Journal,* **10**(3), 111–28.

Ganschow, L. and Schneider E. (1997) 'Teaching all students: from research to reality', in Vogely, A. J. (ed.) *Celebrating Languages, Opening All Minds!* Proceedings of the New York State Association of Foreign Language Teachers. Annual Meeting Series No.14, pp. 89–96.

Ganschow, L. and Sparks, R. (1995) 'Effects of direct instruction in phonology on the native skills and foreign aptitude of at-risk foreign language learners'. *Journal of Learning Disabilities*, **28**, 107–20.

Ganschow, L., Sparks, R. and Javorksy, J. (1998) 'Foreign language learning difficulties: a historical perspective'. *Journal of Learning Disabilities*, **31**, 248–58.

Ganschow, L., Sparks, R. and Schneider, E. (1995) 'Learning a foreign language: challenges for students with language learning difficulties'. *Dyslexia: International Journal of Research and Practice*, **1**, 75–95.

Gerber, A. (1993a) (ed.) *Language-related Learning Disabilities: Their Nature and Treatment.* Baltimore, MD: Paul Brookes Publishing.

Hickey, K. (2000) *A Language Course for Teachers and Learners.* London: Elisabeth Arnolds.

Hill, B., Downey, D. M., Sheppard, M. and Williamson, V. (1995) 'Accommodating the needs of students with severe language learning difficulties in modified foreign language classes', in Crouse, G. K., Campana, P. J. and Rosenbusch, M. H. (eds) *Broadening the Frontiers of Foreign Language Education.* Selected Papers from the 1995 Central States Conference. Lincolnwood, IL: National Textbook Company, pp. 46–56.

Javorsky, J., Sparks, R. and Ganschow, L. (1992) 'Perceptions of college students with and without specific learning disabilities about foreign language courses'. *Learning Disabilities Research and Practice*, **7**, 31–44.

Kenneweg, S. (1988) 'Meeting special learning needs in the Spanish curriculum at a college preparatory school', in Snyder, B. (ed.) *Get Ready, Set, Go! Action in the Foreign Language Classroom.* Columbus, OH: Ohio Foreign Language Association, pp. 16–18.

Krashen, S. (1987) *Principles and Practice in Second Language Acquisition.* Oxford: Oxford University Press.

Lerner, J. (1997) *Learning Disabilities: Theories, Diagnosis and Teaching Strategies.* Boston, MA: Houghton Mifflin.

MacIntyre, P. and Gardner, R. (1994a) 'The subtle effects of language anxiety on cognitive processing in the second language'. *Language Learning*, **44**, 283–305.

MacIntyre, P. and Gardner (1994b) 'Toward a social psychological model of strategy use'. *Foreign Language Annals*, **27**, 185–95.

MacIntyre, P. and Gardner, R. (1995) 'How does anxiety affect second language learning? A reply to Sparks and Ganschow'. *Modern Language Journal*, **79**, 1–32.

Mastropieri, M. and Scruggs, T. (1991) *Teaching Students Ways to Remember: Strategies for Learning Mnemonically.* Newton, MA: Brookline Publishers.

Miles, E. (1989) *The Bangor Dyslexia Teaching System.* London: Whurr Publishers.

Miles, T. R. (1993) *Dyslexia: The Pattern of Difficulties* (2nd edn). London: Whurr Publishers.

Miles, T. R. and Miles, E. (1999) *Dyslexia: A Hundred Years On* (2nd edn). Milton Keynes: Open University Press.

Palincsar, A. S. and Brown, D. A. (1987) 'Enhancing instructional time through attention in metacognition'. *Journal of Learning Disabilities*, **20**, 66–75.

Perani, D. *et al.* (1996) 'Brain processing of native and foreign languages'. *NeuroReport*, **7**, 2439–44.

Perspectives: Study and Organization Skills (Special Issue) (2003) International Dyslexia Association quarterly publication, Baltimore, MD, Winter.

Pintrich, P. R., Marx, R. W. and Boyle, R. A. (1993) 'Beyond cold conceptual change: the role of motivational beliefs and classroom contextual factors in the process of conceptual change'. *Review of Educational Research*, **63**, 67–199.

Pressley, M. (2002) *Reading Instruction that Works* (2nd edn). New York: Guilford Press.

Pressley, M. and Woloshyn, V. (1995) *Cognitive Strategy Instruction that Really Improves Children's Academic Performance.* Newton, MA: Brookline Publishers.

Rome, P. and Osman, J. (2002) *The English Language Tool Kit and Manual.* Cambridge, MA: Educators Publishing.

Schneider, E. (1999) *Multisensory Structured Metacognitive Instruction: An Approach to Teaching a Foreign Language to At-risk Students.* Frankfurt a. M., Germany: Peter Lang Verlag.

Schneider, E. and Ganschow, L. (2000) 'Dynamic assessment and teaching of learners who struggle to learn a foreign language'. *Dyslexia: International Journal of Research and Practice*, **6**, 72–82.

Schneider, E. and Philips, L. (1999) *Nick's Story: A LD Student's Success Story in a College Foreign Language Course.* Oxford, OH: Miami University, Media Center Production (producer

Gregg Rousse) (unpublished video documentary).

Scruggs, T. and Mastropieri, M. (1992) *Teaching Test Taking Skills: Helping Students Show What They Know.* Newton, MA: Brookline Publishers.

Sparks, R. and Miller, K. (2000) 'Teaching a foreign language using multisensory structured language techniques to at-risk learners: a review'. *Dyslexia*, **6**, 124–32.

Sperber, H. G. (1989) *Mnemotechniken im Fremdsprachenunterricht mit Schwerpunkt 'Deutsch als Fremdsprache'*, **9** (Studien Deutsch), in Krusche, D. and Weinrich, H. (eds) Munich, Germany: Iudicium Verlag.

Stanovich, K. E. and Siegel, L. (1994) 'Phenotype performance profile of children with reading disabilities: a regression-based test of the phonological core variable differences model'. *Journal of Educational Psychology*, **86**, 24–53.

Thomas, S. *et al.* (1991–2003) *MLG Games.* London: MLG Publishing.

Van Kleeck, A. (1994) 'Metalinguistic development', in Wallach, G. P. and Butler K. G. (eds) *Language Learning Disabilities in School-age Children and Adolescents: Some Principles and Applications.* New York: MacMillan College Publishing Company, pp. 53–98.

West, T. G. (1991) *In the Mind's Eye.* New York: Prometheus Books.

Wong, B. Y. L., Wong R., Perry N. and Squatzky, D. (1986) 'The efficacy of a self-questioning summarization strategy for use by underachievers and learning disabled adolescents in social studies'. *Learning Disability Focus*, **2**, 20–35.

Yaden, B. and Templeton, S. (1986) (eds) *Metalinguistic Awareness and Beginning Literacy: Conceptualizing what it Means to Read and Write.* Portsmouth, NH: Heinemann.

Yopp, H. K. (1992) 'Phonemic awareness in young children'. *The Reading Teacher*, **45**, 696–703.

Index